RESTRICTED NATIONS

NIGERIA

ADVANCING GOD'S KINGDOM IN THE CALIPHATE

The Voice of the Martyrs

with Dr. Roy Stults and Kameron Nettleton

RESTRICTED
NATIONS

Nigeria: Advancing God's Kingdom in the Caliphate

VOM Books
P.O. Box 443
Bartlesville, OK 74005-0443

© 2015 by The Voice of the Martyrs. All rights reserved. No part of this book may be reproduced, stored in a retrieval system, or transmitted in any form or by any means, except in the case of brief quotations printed in articles or reviews, without prior permission in writing from the publisher.

ISBN 978-0-88264-149-2

Edited by Lynn Copeland

Cover design by Lookout Design

Page design and layout by Genesis Group

Printed in the United States of America

Unless otherwise indicated, Scripture references are from the *New King James* version, © 1979, 1980, 1982 by Thomas Nelson Inc., Publishers, Nashville, Tennessee.

NIGERIA

> *"You Christians should know that Jesus . . . is not the son of God. This religion of Christianity you are practicing is not a religion of God—it is paganism. We are trying to coerce you to embrace Islam, because that is what [Allah] instructed us to do."*
>
> —ABUBAKAR SHEKAU,
> leader of the radical Muslim group Boko Haram,
> who in 2010 declared war on Christians

RESTRICTED NATIONS

"Remember the word that I said to you, 'A servant is not greater than his master.' If they persecuted Me, they will also persecute you."

—JESUS CHRIST (John 15:20)

NIGERIA

CONTENTS

Acknowledgments 6

Faith Amid the Fire 7

Facts about Nigeria 12

Nigeria: On the World Stage 14

The Early History of Islam in Nigeria 23

A Fulani Convert: A Vessel to His Own People ..30

The Early History of Christianity in Nigeria 34

Political Unrest and Religious Violence:
2011 Post-election Riots 48

Handing Everything to God 55

Nigeria Deals with Shariah 57

Testimony: Responding Like Jesus 64

Bad Meat, Bad Blood 66

Prosthetic Limbs for Persecuted Christians 69

Boko Haram, Ansaru, and Fulani Herdsmen:
Present-day Persecutors 74

Two Girls Escape Boko Haram 96

Hated by All but Called by God 98

Hope in the Midst of Hardship 104

*Words of Forgiveness from
Persecuted Christians* 108

For Further Reading 109

Resources 111

ACKNOWLEDGMENTS

Kameron Nettleton began the work on this book, providing me with good resources and informative material, and Dory P. has added material to it, allowing the book to be well-rounded with factual information and personal stories.

I appreciate the opportunity The Voice of the Martyrs has given me to be able to research and write this book. It has been very enlightening. Before I began this project I knew only what I had heard in the news and it was not always good. The stories of Samuel Crowther and Mary Slessor were especially inspiring. It seems that evil seeks to destroy those persons and places that have the greatest potential for the kingdom of God. Nigeria has tremendous potential and the suffering they are enduring for Christ makes them powerful examples of steadfastness and faithfulness. It is an encouragement to the global church.

DR. ROY STULTS

NIGERIA

FAITH AMID THE FIRE

The sound of shouts and gunshots near the compound that included his house and church alarmed Pastor John Ali Doro. In the early morning hours, he heard people yelling warnings that a group of Muslims was approaching.

It was July 7, 2012, and the Fulani, a mostly Muslim ethnic group who raise cattle in Nigeria, were attacking nearby Christian villages and closing in on Pastor John's village of Maseh. Relations between the Christians and the Fulani were usually peaceful and even friendly, but on this day that was all forgotten. Dressed in black and armed with automatic weapons, the Fulani wanted the Christians to leave so they could take over their land. Pastor John knew that it would not take the mob long to reach the village that he and his wife and children called home.

Unlike most Saturdays, Pastor John had not gone out to the farm early in the morning. This change in his routine became part of God's saving grace. The attackers approached Maseh from the direction of his farm. They surely would have killed him if they had found him out there all alone.

Moments before the Fulani arrived, Pastor John dived into a ditch to conceal himself from the armed attackers who were surrounding the church. They were shooting any Christians they saw outside the building, including those trying to flee. Others huddled inside the church, screaming for help.

RESTRICTED NATIONS

Pastor John lay in the ditch, shocked and terrified by what he was seeing. It seemed like a dream. He knew that if he ran to the building to try to save those inside, he would be running to his death. He could do nothing but pray and endure the screams of those who had taken shelter inside the church.

Pastor John watched in horror as the attackers began to set the building on fire. *"Allahu Akbar! Allahu Akbar!"* ("God is great!") shouted the Fulani attackers over and over. The Muslim chant was mingled with the screams and cries of the believers trapped in the burning building. The pastor was close enough to hear several of the Fulani gloating and taunting the Christians inside. "Let's see if their God can save them," they mocked.

Nine other Christian villages were attacked on the same day. It wasn't until the Nigerian Special Forces arrived that the Fulani were driven back from their vicious assault. The troops were too late to save the forty-four people in John's village who perished, in-

Pastor John lost his family to terrorist attacks.

cluding his wife, four of his seven children, and two of his grandsons. The children were ages five to eighteen.

Unfortunately, the attackers weren't finished and the bloodshed was far from over.

On the following day, as the villagers tried to bury the bodies of their fallen neighbors in a mass funeral, the Fulani returned and attacked again. Many of those who had managed to escape the wrath of the Fulani on the previous day were killed in the second attack. Several government officials were present at the funeral—a factor which may have drawn the Fulani out again—and a national senator and a member of the Plateau State Assembly House were killed. Over the two-day period, almost two hundred Christians were murdered.

Pastor John had lived in Maseh for five years before the attacks occurred. In all his time there, the relationship had been peaceful between the Christian villagers and the Muslim herdsmen who were their neighbors. They had lived side by side without issue. Something changed, however, and Pastor John believes the attacks were pre-planned attempts to completely rid the area of Christians. He believes this was *jihad*, a war declared on non-Muslims. He has been told that the al-Qaeda–linked radical Islamic presence in Nigeria is headquartered among the Fulani herdsmen. He believes that the extremist views of radical Islam influenced the Fulani to attack.

In response to the second attack, the Nigerian government ordered the Christians in the area to temporarily evacuate so that they could deal with the insurgents. The troops they promised were never sent, however. The Fulani herdsmen who attacked Maseh and the surrounding villages still live in the area, while many of the Christians who evacuated have not returned. On one hand, they fear more attacks if they go back. Some believers returned to try to harvest the crops they had planted before leaving, and they were met with more gunfire from the Fulani. On the other hand, the Fulani did not leave much for them to return to. Pastor John said the Fulani burned the homes and then tore the bricks down, completely leveling the buildings.

When asked by a VOM associate how he was able to deal with the tragic loss of his family, Pastor John says that he is strengthened by the biblical account of Job, who also lost his family and earthly possessions. He is especially drawn to Job 2:9,10. "Job's wife told him to curse God and die," Pastor John said. "But his reply was that in the days when there is good from the Lord, we accept it. When there is difficulty, how will we refuse to accept that? That verse encourages me. I draw strength from that."

Since the attack, Pastor John has moved to another village and continues his work as pastor. He still lives in the same area near the Fulani who attacked his village, and sometimes he will see

NIGERIA

them in the village he now resides in. Through the grace of God, he has forgiven the attackers who took his family from him, and he says that he is open to talking to them and demonstrating godly kindness toward them. Many of the men who were involved in the attack cross the street if they see Pastor John walking toward them. They are afraid to face him. Pastor John hopes he will have the opportunity someday to speak to the men and lead them to Christ.

FACTS ABOUT NIGERIA

Nigeria today is a federal constitutional republic (the Federal Republic of Nigeria) with a powerful influence in Western Africa. Some other facts about Nigeria include the following:

- It is composed of thirty-six states and a federal capital territory.
- With the largest population of any African nation, it is twice the size of California geographically, and it is the seventh most populous country in the world with 140 million people.
- It is home to over five hundred ethnic groups (figures vary) with the three largest being the Hausa (and Fulani), Igbo, and Yoruba. The rivalry among these ethnic groups has dominated Nigeria's politics, with the Fulani and the Hausa competing for power in the pre-colonial era.
- The nation boasts fertile agricultural land and vast oil resources.
- Nigeria has the second largest economy in Africa and is currently the thirty-seventh largest in the world.
- The Christian population is roughly equal to the Muslim population in the country, and the close proximity of the two ideologically different groups is a near-constant source of tension.

NIGERIA

- Most of the nation's 80 million Christians live in the south with a Christian culture that favors mega-churches and prosperity preachers, while the north has been predominantly Islamic for centuries and is where a radical Islamic culture, characterized by massive riots, bombings, and a plan to create an Islamic state, is most evident.
- There are many millions of Christians in the Muslim-majority north and many millions of Muslims in the Christian-majority south.
- The middle of the country, called the Middle Belt, is where much of the violence occurs, although it is not isolated to that area by any means.
- Religious violence is common, and Nigeria's short history as a united nation is marred with brutal religious riots that devastate entire regions.

RESTRICTED NATIONS

NIGERIA: ON THE WORLD STAGE

Nigeria is a country that cannot be ignored. Its difficult history of serious intra-ethnic and religious conflicts and its important role in Africa bring it to the attention of the world on a regular basis. Western countries, particularly Britain, became very interested in the region in the late nineteenth century. The nation's vast oil resources and the rise of radical Islam keep it in the spotlight in the twenty-first century.

Early Nigerian history shows the population was largely defined by village bonds and ethnic communities, with the rise of various states and kingdoms prior to the partitioning of Africa by Europeans nations in 1900. Early trade routes brought Arab and Berber merchants to the area. The Berbers largely converted to Islam, with the benefit that they could not be made slaves by Muslim slave traders. The merchants were educated and served in the courts of various kingdoms. Spanish and Portuguese explorers and merchants in the sixteenth century were the first Europeans to trade in Nigeria, dealing in goods as well as participating in the slave trade. Slavery had been a part of the African scene for centuries. People who were captured in war by various tribal and ethnic groups were made slaves, taken back to the conqueror's homeland for labor, and sometimes absorbed into the culture. In the early nine-

NIGERIA

teenth century the slave trade changed when, with the help of some European countries, slaves from Africa were sent to the Caribbean and to the Americas as laborers.

The Fulani Empire dates from the beginning of the nineteenth century until Africa was partitioned. The partitioning was a process beginning in the 1880s and was finally completed in 1900. Britain and France were the major players in colonizing West Africa. The colonial era in Nigeria officially began in 1900 with the British trying to unify Nigeria and administer it through both direct and indirect rule, but Britain's influence had been felt since the early part of the nineteenth century and gradually gained prominence. When Great Britain abolished slavery in 1807, they tried to halt the slave trade in Africa, and would intercept slave ships and take the freed slaves to Sierra Leone. This would prove to be a strategic move in the evangelism of West Africa.

By 1855 Britain's claim to West Africa was recognized by other nations. The Royal Niger Company, a mercantile company, was formed in 1879 to govern and carry on commerce in West Africa, leading to the formation of colonial Nigeria. Their land eventually came under the control of the British government and led to what now constitutes modern Nigeria. Independent kingdoms fought the British in the late nineteenth and early twentieth centuries to try to throw off British rule but they were ultimately defeated. By 1900, the partitioning of Africa by European nations was completed. In 1914, the two protectorates, Northern Nigeria and Southern Nigeria, were amalgamated by the British under Sir Frederick Lugard, and the united area was called Nigeria.

The Partitioning of Africa

The partitioning of Africa by European nations ignored cultural, ethnic, and political boundaries set up by Africans that had existed for centuries. This created many ongoing difficulties as various ethnic and religious groups jostled for power or equality in the context of their new geographical boundaries. Conflicts are always provoked by several interrelated and complex factors. Often the majority of a particular ethnic group embraces one religion, so conflict with other groups can be both tribal and religious. Since Nigeria was artificially created, observers wondered if it would survive as a nation. It has survived but not without many significant struggles.

The Attempt to Unify Nigeria

In 1914, when the British unified the two independent states into one colonial Nigeria, the southern part of the country was to be governed by direct rule of the British. The northern portion of the colony was governed by indirect rule; the local power structure was allowed to remain mostly intact, so long as those in power submitted to British authority. Governed by a Muslim Caliphate,

NIGERIA

this opened the door for many of the northern states to adopt Shariah law, the moral and religious code of Islam. Caliphate means "succession" and refers to an Islamic state led by a supreme religious/political leader, a caliph or successor (to Mohammad or other Islamic leaders and prophets). The north became a breeding ground for radical Muslim movements. This method of governance would create serious issues in north/south relations in the future and greater difficulty in truly unifying the country.

The Caliphate in the north, it appears, used *jihad* to promote and justify slavery and colonization by Muslims. Unifying the states into one colony began the slow process of Nigeria becoming one country, as the different autonomous tribes and their leaders were unified under one rule. To accomplish this, Nigerians needed to transition from loyalty to village and tribe to embrace the idea of loyalty to their nation. Michael Crowder, a distinguished British historian who has written volumes on West African and Nigerian history, believes that missionary activity helped to foster and strengthen nationalism—partly because Nigerians rejected missionary attempts to destroy African culture and partly because of the Christian ideal of the equality of all persons. Colonial rule played a part in attempting to unify the country by giving the various tribes and ethnic groups a common language, law, trade, and administration. It fostered a sense of unity and nation-

RESTRICTED NATIONS

hood, but real national unity has, even now, eluded Nigerians.

Lingering Divisions

Despite the geographical unification, the nation remained drastically divided both religiously and ethnically. Religion can have a unifying effect, uniting persons of one particular religion, as well as a divisive effect, causing division on the national scene. The south, where the British influence had been strongest, has a large Christian population, and more similarities to a European way of life. This is not so in the north, where traditional religions and Islamic beliefs have largely been the norm and remain so today.

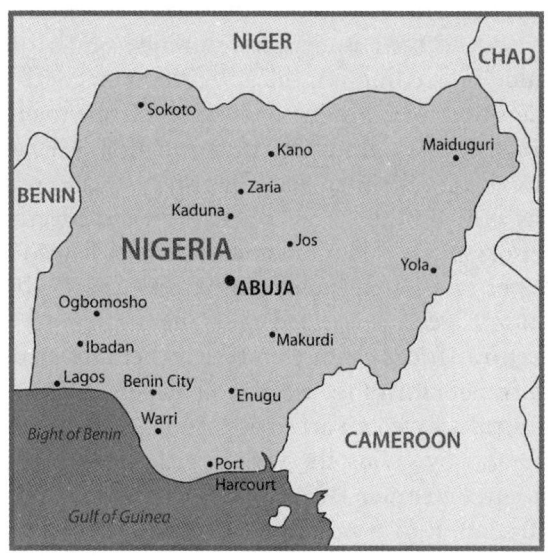

NIGERIA

As time went on, there was a push in the country for independence from colonial rule. In the early 1950s, Nigerian leaders convened a conference and assembled the framework of what an independent Nigeria would look like. On October 1, 1960, after petitioning for complete independence for decades, Nigeria was made a fully sovereign state of the British Commonwealth. Tafawa Balewa, the first Prime Minister of independent Nigeria, declared that day that "Nigeria now stands well built upon firm foundations." While gaining independence was a big step for the country, it was not without difficulties. The history of Nigeria shows a nation struggling to define the way it would function. Nigerian leaders adopted a constitution and declared the nation a federated republic with a multi-level political system similar to that of the United States. However, the foundation that Balewa spoke so highly of was not as firm as he praised it to be. Regional and religious divisions were both key issues that would be a factor in the country's politics for years. Great debate surrounded the adoption of the constitution with Muslims pressing for Shariah to be adopted as the law of the land. For the next three decades Nigeria suffered under several military coups. It finally turned into a civil war, torn by regional and ethnic interests.

RESTRICTED NATIONS

The Nigerian Civil War
It the late 1960s, people in the region of Biafra attempted to gain independence but the failed effort cost the lives of up to three million people due to disease, starvation, and strife. In the southeast region of Nigeria, the Igbo people were predominantly Roman Catholics and practiced democracy quite successfully. Unhappy with how the country was developing, they declared themselves the independent Republic of Biafra. After a failed attempt by the government to institute peace, the civil war broke out in 1967, which to the Nigerian government was mostly a "police action" intended to end quickly. However, to the leader of the Igbo people, Colonel Odumegwu Ojukwu, it was far more serious—it was an attempt by the Nigerian government to eradicate the Igbo people from the land. The fighting lasted two and a half years and resulted in the collapse and surrender of the Republic of Biafra. The war was prolonged because Biafra was aided by several nations concerned with the reports of genocide. The grave human suffering resulted in the death of millions from starvation, illness, and exposure. Eventually the conflict did end, although it left a lot of scars on the young nation.

The Nigerian Civil War, while not directly a religious war, appeared to have religious implications, as do most conflicts in Nigeria. Politically speaking, however, the war was the result of several different groups seeking to gain power and control over the young country. The Nigerian Civil War threatened to tear Nigeria, less than a decade old, into pieces and had serious consequences for the struggling nation. The end of the war brought an end to the bloodshed, but great damage had been done.

A Time of Instability and the New Democracy
Nigeria's political situation remained unstable at best and at war's end, the most important political power in Nigeria was the military. The standing army had grown enormously during the war, and military officials realized that they held the majority of power in the nation as it attempted to rebuild and repair the fractured relationships. The continued political instability led to political and religious riots protesting military rule, further devastating cities and even entire regions. In 1979, Sheu Shagari was elected president, with Nigeria returning to civilian rule. But it was short lived. In 1983 he was deposed by military coup and a second coup took place in 1985.

Religious tension continued to be at the center of many of the problems Nigerians faced during this period. Christians were often targeted by Muslim extremists, who started riots that took hundreds of lives and destroyed much property. These riots were hugely disruptive to the country that was already struggling to find its way and maintain its stability. Nigerians found themselves often divided against their fellow countrymen for

RESTRICTED NATIONS

religious or ethnic reasons, and this division spread all the way to the top of the Nigerian government.

It was not until 1999 that Nigeria regained democracy, ending thirty-three years of military rule. Olusegun Obasanjo served as the military ruler of Nigeria in the late 1970s but was democratically elected president in 1999. He served two terms, overseeing the election of 2007 when Umaru Musa Yar'Adua (a Muslim) came to power, also as a democratically elected president. The vice president, Goodluck Jonathan, was a Christian. Yar'Adua died on May 5, 2010, and Jonathan was sworn in as president the next day. He chose Namadi Sambo, a Muslim, as his vice president. Jonathan was reelected in April 2011 and remains the president today.

NIGERIA

THE EARLY HISTORY OF ISLAM IN NIGERIA

Much of the religious, political, and ethnic conflict in Nigeria's north and Middle Belt finds its roots in the pre-colonial era. The intra-Muslim conflicts and struggles have never been resolved and continue today, often in radical and violent forms. In many ways the pre-colonial Islamic legal traditions and political successes are seen as the Golden Age of Islam in Nigeria, and much of the current struggle is toward a return to this idealized era.

The first documentation of Islam in Nigeria is in the ninth century. It is reported to have been adopted by many leading figures of the Borno Empire during the reign of King Idris Alooma (1571–1603), although many in the empire still held to traditional Nigerian religions.

In the early nineteenth century an elderly Islamic scholar, Usman dan Fodio, became the leader of a *jihad* against the Hausa kingdoms of northern Nigeria. An ethnic Fulani, he was victorious in his *jihad* and established the Fulani Empire with its capital at Sokoto. This became the Sokoto Caliphate, and it also became an ideal model of an Islamic state.

Usman dan Fodio (1754–1817) was an interesting figure. Many Fulani herdsmen had become proselytes of Islam and settled in cities in Hausaland, where they were known as the intellectuals.

Many became wealthy. They sought religious and intellectual reform, something that was worrisome to local Hausa leaders. Fulani Muslims, particularly dan Fodio, criticized religious laxity and the decadent standards for learning in the Hausa states. There was general unrest among the urban Fulani, and the responsibility for resolving it was placed upon Usman dan Fodio, then an elderly Muslim scholar, who was also an urban Fulani.

Dan Fodio was well-educated in classical Islamic science (philosophy and theology) and he became a revered religious teacher of the Maliki school of law. While he was a young man he moved to Degel, where he studied the Qur'an with his father. Later, he went to live and study with other relatives who were scholars, which was the traditional way of traveling from teacher to teacher and studying Islamic subjects. A teacher from the southern Saharan city of Agadez, Jibril ibn 'Umar, had a powerful intellectual and religious influence on him. 'Umar taught that it was the duty (and within the power) of religious reform movements to establish an ideal society free of vice and oppression. In his studies dan Fodio came into contact with reformist ideas that were stirring in the Muslim world at that time. He got the government's approval to create a religious community in his hometown of Degel, where he hoped to create a model Islamic town as envisioned by his teachers. He sought to create an Islamic theocratic state based on a stricter interpretation of Islam, which would be done through Shariah.

In the 1780s and 1790s dan Fodio's reputation increased exponentially and the community looked to him for both political and religious leadership. The economic and social grievances of the day spawned millenarian hopes of bringing about a glorious golden age of Islam (similar to the Christian idea of a millennium). Many began to identify him with the Mahdi, the prophesied redeemer of Islamic eschatology. Dan Fodio rejected this application to himself personally but he did share in the hope and expectations of the rest of the community for the coming of the Mahdi.

Dan Fodio criticized the African Muslim elites and leadership for their tolerance of paganism and for their greed, which he thought violated the standards of Shariah. He denounced the Muslim leaders for returning, at least in part, to paganism, usually to placate those in their kingdoms who held to traditional religions. To be politically expedient, they created a "calculated syncretism," a blending of Islam with the traditional religions, which they believed helped them to maintain rule over all the people.

The Hausa rulers saw the Fulani attack on paganism as a threat to their authority, and they forced dan Fodio from the court where he was a respected scholar. The sultan Nafata, a ruler in the city-state of Gobir (Gobirwa), became alarmed at the growing influence of the Degel community and feared that dan Fodio was creating a state within a state. Degel is a town in northern Nigeria that was once a part of the Hausa city-state of Gobir and was the home of the Fulani Islamic reformer dan Fodio. Consequently, he proclaimed that no Shaykh (Sheikh, or religious leader, as dan Fodio came to be called) could preach, their sons were forbidden to convert from the religion of their fathers (which appeared to be in support of traditional religions and protection from Muslim proselyting), and the wearing of turbans and veils was banned.

Nafata's son, Yunfa, succeeded Nafata as sultan and tried to rid himself of dan Fodio's influence. Though he is thought to have been a pupil of the scholar, he tried to kill him but did not succeed. Dan Fodio prevailed and set up the Sokoto Caliphate that became an ideal for later Islamic reform movements. When dan Fodio retired, he handed the leadership over to his son, Islamic scholar Mohammed Bello (1814–1836), and to his brother, Abdullahi.

In 1809, Sokoto would become the key capital for his father's conquest of Hausa lands in the Fulani War (1804–1810). As the sultan of the Fulani Empire and the Sokoto Caliphate, Bello carried on his father's legacy by spreading Islam throughout the region. He established Islamic courts and provided educational opportunities for both men and women, in keeping with his father's desire that women have more participation in society. The Sokoto Caliphate was one of the largest and most powerful states in all of Africa, and included the large populations of Fulani and Hausa peoples.

**Muslims Fighting Muslims:
The Rise of Reformist Movements**
Since Islamic orthodoxy forbids making war against fellow Muslims, one way of bypassing this doctrine is to declare that the person you wish to fight is an apostate; then you can subsequently declare a *jihad* against him. The sultan of Gobir, for example, fearing that dan Fodio would set up a rival caliphate, called dan Fodio an apostate and attacked him and his followers, which amounted to Muslim fighting Muslims. As a result of this attack, dan Fodio declared a *jihad* against all Hausa rulers and one by one they lost their thrones, allowing him to establish Fulani control over most of northern Nigeria. *Jihad* became increasingly political during this time, but in the Muslim mind, this was not a contradiction; religion and politics go hand in hand.

There were many reformist movements leading up to and even during dan Fodio's *jihad*. Most were seeking a return to the pure and primitive faith of Islam, being purged of all heresies, breaking with the practice of syncretism with traditional religions and other additions to the primitive faith. The desire was to go back to the original model of the Islamic state during the time of the

Prophet Mohammad and the first four caliphs. They believed this would create a state of social justice precipitated and dictated by Shariah at the hands of God-fearing rulers. So war against other Muslims who co-mingled other religions and ideas with Islam was justified. Many of the themes of this era would simmer and resurface later in the radical Muslim movements in the 1980s onward.

In reformist movements in post-colonial days and the late nineteenth century, another theme that is often echoed (and that resurfaces in Nigeria today) is the Islamic belief in the failure of Western civilization, especially after the Enlightenment, to appreciate the role of religion in society. Western culture has tried, through the secularist agenda, to do away with religion (especially Christianity) and religious influence in Western society, delegating it to purely a private, personal affair, inappropriate in the public square.

Islamic scholars, especially those deemed "fundamentalists," believe the Islamic religion is very much a part of the governance of society and is the basis for social norms and functions. Islam has been a part of the social and political scene in Nigeria for centuries and should play, they believe, an increasing role in the future. Their vision is for an Islamic state based on Shariah and they have mounted a *jihad* against modernism, which they equate with Western secular influence.

Since Christianity has been viewed as a tool of Western influence, Nigerian Islamists believe it should be eradicated from Nigerian society along with all evidences of Western influence and decadence. This is the basis of much of the persecution against Christians. It is an irrational view of Christianity, since Christianity originated in the Middle East and was carried to Nigeria predominantly by Africans. They equate any change in the idealistic Islamic way as an aberration and automatically blame it on the West, when in reality much of the change in Islam has come from within Islam itself. Islam is not a monolithic religious unity but is made up of many sects and branches and denominations, with intense rivalries that have led to wars among themselves.

The World is Watching
With the eyes of the world on Nigeria, the resilience of the Nigerian church can be seen now more than ever before. God will use the difficult circumstances and suffering of the Nigerian Christians to glorify His name and bring people to Him. Among those who come to Him during this time of persecution will be some of the persecutors. That is our prayer.

A FULANI CONVERT: A VESSEL TO HIS OWN PEOPLE

It's always amazing to hear about God's ability to transform the lives of those who have hated Him and fought against Him. The story of Abdullahi Ishaku's encounter with the Lord reminds one of Saul of Tarsus: a man once trained to kill Christians found Christ, and his passion is now not to kill but to reach his own people with the gospel he once repelled. Born in 1979 in Gombe State into a rich Fulani clan, the famous Sokoto Caliphate, Abdullahi Ishaku was taught in several Arabic and Qur'anic schools in Nigeria and Saudi Arabia.

The Fulani are a large ethnic group of about forty million people with a common language, Fulfulde, that are geographically and culturally diverse primarily in West Africa and the northern parts of Central Africa. They are traditionally Muslims and many are herdsmen, moving large numbers of livestock as they pursue water and grazing for their animals. In Nigeria, the Fulani defeated the Hausa in a holy war that began in 1804, and they subsequently adopted the Hausa language and consolidated the ruling classes of both groups to form the Hausa-Fulani ethnic that became the Sokoto Caliphate. It is the Fulani herdsmen who are now raiding Christian villages and killing people. A few years ago they killed around five hundred people in the Dogo-Nahawa

NIGERIA

village, including women and children (thirty-three infants and children under age five).

Anyone wanting to evangelize the Fulani people would need to have a special connection with them, and none would be better than one of their own. The Lord provided for Himself a ready vessel, a person who once was a hardened, fanatical Muslim.

Seeking to be one of the Fulani warriors to defend Islam, Ishaku traveled to Saudi Arabia where he was trained in how to defend the Islamic religion at all costs. When he returned to Nigeria, he was a fanatical Muslim, attending various Arabic and Islamic schools to attain higher education in Islam. As a son of a wealthy Fulani father, he was able to pay for various training camps where he continued his training in fighting and defending Islam. "I had inherited many cows from my father, and within a few years, I had raised so many herds of cattle that I could donate money to support any Islamic course," Ishaku confessed.

"On one fateful day, we decided to attack a particular village because the community did not want our cattle to graze freely on their farmland. It was after these attacks that some of us were arrested and put into prison," he explains.

Ishaku's Conversion

While he was in prison, a woman would visit regularly to evangelize the inmates. In one of her visits she mentioned that God is able to set them free

RESTRICTED NATIONS

from their present condition. It struck a chord in Ishaku's heart. "That night," he explains, "I prayed asking God to make a way for me to go out of this torment and I will surrender my life to Him. It was barely a month later when I and a few other inmates were released after having spent over three years in prison."

On the day of his release, the female evangelist was also present, and as she ministered to the prisoners Ishaku made a decision. "I surrendered my life to Christ," he testifies. After many sessions of prayer, counseling, and follow-up to his decision, he was directed to a discipleship ministry to properly educate and watch over him so he could become grounded in his newfound faith.

"When my family finally found out that I was released from the prison and had now become a Christian, they said they would try to kill me but they did not succeed. The ministry decided to send me to be trained in a Bible school where my family could not locate me," he adds.

Abdullahi Ishaku, Fulani convert

After returning from the Bible training school, Ishaku met with representatives of The Voice of the Martyrs (VOM), where he learned of the Fulani Mp3 audio Bible project. Christian workers are distributing 10,000 Mp3 players with audio Bibles, enabling many traditionally Muslim Fulani people in northeastern Nigeria to hear the gospel for the first time through these resources. The project captivated his heart because of its ability to reach his people with the gospel. He traveled to several Fulani settlements to distribute the audio Bible and he felt that it was a very effective tool.

Ishaku's Call
Ishaku was moved to answer the call for a fulltime Fulani worker to serve on one of the Fulani fields. He agreed to move his family—a wife and five children—from Jos to join the team of workers in the field. According to Ishaku, his desire is to join hands with a ministry that is reaching out to the Fulanis with the gospel of salvation, and this was an opportunity that he could not pass up.

THE EARLY HISTORY OF CHRISTIANITY IN NIGERIA

The earliest attempts to reach Nigeria for Christ have had both positive and negative effects on the work of the church in Nigeria even to this day. Though the attempts facilitated the work of evangelism to non-Muslims in the south, they also complicated subsequent efforts to evangelize Muslims in the north. Portuguese traders first introduced Roman Catholicism to West Africa and Nigeria, entering the territory in the 1400s. It died away after two hundred years, but Roman Catholic missionaries returning in the 1800s were able to revive it. Today there are about nineteen million Roman Catholic adherents in Nigeria.

The first Protestants to enter Nigeria were Wesleyan Methodists who began their work in the southwest part of Nigeria with the Yoruba people in 1842. Many groups soon followed, including the Church Missionary Society (evangelical Anglican), United Free Church of Scotland, Southern Baptists, and a host of others for the next fifty years.

The British made an agreement with the Fulani Muslims, who resided in northern Nigeria, that the British and Western missionaries would limit their efforts to southern Nigeria. Early Christianity in Nigeria was centered along the coast, although it did eventually move inward after concerted missionary effort. Islam was already present in the country, especially the northern part of the country. Records of this time in Nigeria's history are light on details, but they are clear that many of the northern tribes were hostile to the Christians who came into the north, and the growth of Christianity stagnated as it went northward. This had lasting effects on the situation in the north and in the relationship of northern states to the rest of the country, and helps to understand the predicament of Christians in the north after Nigeria became an independent nation.

Abolition and the Formation of Mission Societies

The late eighteenth century saw was a time for the formation of many mission societies that would later work in Nigeria. The London Missionary Society was founded in 1795 while the Church Missionary Society was founded in 1799. Earlier the Africa Association (The Association for Promoting the Discovery of the Interior Parts of Africa) was formed in 1788 as a British club dedicated to the exploration of West Africa. They desired scientific knowledge and, the abolition of the slave trade, and were not opposed to finding opportunities to promoted British economic and business interests.

In Britain, The Committee for the Abolition of the Slave Trade was formed in 1787 when a group of Evangelical English Protestants along with Quakers united in their opposition to slavery. On

RESTRICTED NATIONS

March 25, 1807, the British parliament passed The Abolition Act of 1807 that banned Britain from participating in the slave trade, although it did not ban slavery outright. The abolitionists of course assumed that ending the slave trade would eventually lead to the freeing of slaves but when it became clear that this would not happen, Thomas Clarkson and Thomas Fowell Buxton formed The Society for the Mitigation and Gradual Abolition of Slavery (later called the Anti-Slavery Society) in 1823. In May of that year, Buxton introduced a motion in the British House of Commons to end slavery itself, and not just the trafficking in slaves.

This eventually resulted in the passing of the Slavery Abolition Act of 1833, abolishing slavery throughout the British Empire—with certain exceptions, which were later eliminated in 1843. This changed the perspective of the British regarding slavery and they became a force determined to stem the slave trade in West Africa. This had a positive effect on the Christian mission to Africa. The British would intercept and stop ships loaded with slaves from West Africa and would free them, sending many to Sierra Leone, an area created specifically for freed slaves. Some of these freed slaves later became missionaries to Nigeria.

The prevailing idea at the time was to use the manpower of freed slaves to develop Africa, and this was to be done, Western missionaries believed, by cultivating the habits of industry and by preaching the gospel to provide the moral basis for society. Consequently, schools in the south were set up to be agricultural training centers and Christianity was taught as the basis of spiritual regeneration of Africa. Christians in the south also received a formal education that equipped them for trade and relations with the nations of Europe.

Because the south's educational system focused on practical training in skills to support commercial enterprise, the economic situation in the south was much better than it was in the north due to this drastic difference in education. Tribes in the north fell behind economically and educationally, which led to resentment between the two areas. This resentment was just the beginning of a divide between the north and the south, a divide that has only deepened through the years.

Another lasting effect of missions activity was the stark contrast in religious beliefs between Nigerians in the south and the north. Christianity had spread rapidly in the south, becoming an important part of the southern Nigerian culture. The north was more tribal, and many tribes had been influenced by the Muslim beliefs of the people groups surrounding Nigeria. This difference in religion was a source of tension as Nigeria was beginning to take shape as a nation, and it continues to have an impact on the relationship between Christians and Muslims today. Much of the persecution in the nation can be traced back to the resentment that began to grow during the eighteenth century.

Samuel Crowther

One of the freed slaves from Nigeria who was sent to Sierra Leone and eventually returned to Nigeria was Samuel Ajayi Crowther. He was captured by Muslim Fulani slave traders when he was only twelve years old and sold to Portuguese slave traders, but the ship that he was on was boarded by the British Navy. Crowther was freed and taken to Sierra Leone, where he received an education. He trusted in Christ around 1825, and became the most widely known and respected African Christian of the nineteenth century.

Crowther was from the town of Ososgun in Yorubaland (now in southwestern Nigeria). He wrote later that about three years after his liberation from human slavery, he was convinced that there was a worse state of slavery, that of Satan and sin. He was baptized "into the visible Church of Christ" so he could fight the spiritual battle with unseen enemies. He was baptized by John Raban of the Church Missionary Society (Anglican) and he took the name of one of their members, Samuel Crowther. Later, after the conversion of his mother, he was able to baptize her and she chose the name Hannah, the mother of the prophet Samuel.

Crowther had a heart for his people as well as a great affinity for linguistics. Raban realized that

NIGERIA

Yoruba, Crowther's mother tongue, was a major language in that region. Crowther went to England in 1826 to further his studies before returning to Africa a year later, where he began attending an English school that had been established for education and evangelism. Upon the completion of his studies, he became a teacher at the school. He eventually married a convert Asano (Hassan), formerly a Muslim, who was also on the Portuguese slave ship that originally brought Crowther to Sierra Leone. She chose the name Susana at her baptism and she became a schoolmistress.

In 1841, Crowther was chosen to accompany an English expedition that included German missionary James Frederick Schön into the heart of Nigeria. Schön was renowned for his linguistic work, especially in the Hausa language, and he later would publish both a grammar and a dictionary of the Hausa language. Schön would eventually receive an honorary doctorate from Oxford University for his linguistic work.

Crowther's language skills were considered invaluable to the group, who sought to increase trade and evangelism in the northern parts of the land. The group planned to sail up the Niger River and to map and explore the lands they came across. Other expeditions had been attempted in the past, and the English hoped that they would finally find success. Unfortunately, the expedition failed dramatically, as one-third of the people on board died of malaria. Of the 145 Europeans, all but 15 contracted malaria and 40 eventually died. This failure was a final straw for the English, and most of the future missionary expeditions would be led by Nigerians instead of Englishmen.

Despite the expedition's failure, Crowther was commended for his role, and the following year he was sent to London where he was trained as a minister and ordained by the bishop of London as a priest of the Anglican Church. He returned to Nigeria in 1843 and opened a mission in Abeokuta, along with fellow missionary Henry Townsend, in today's Ogun State.

Many of the tribes in the interior of Nigeria were hostile toward Christian missionaries, and although he was initially met with resistance from the locals, eventually the mission was established and became a base of operations for Crowther's work. From this area, Crowther was able to evangelize and educate many of the local tribes that had not been reached effectively before. Instead of using English in the church as they had done in Sierra Leone, they decided

Samuel Crowther was the first African Anglican bishop in Nigeria.

NIGERIA

to use the Yoruba language. With linguistics as one of his passions, Crowther set to work translating the Bible into the Yoruba language and compiling a dictionary to accompany it. In 1843 he published a grammar book as well, which he had started working on during the Niger mission. His translation of the Bible into the Yoruba language was the first Bible translated into an African language by a native speaker of the language. This was one of the most effective tools of evangelism used in the area. Many Nigerians came to faith directly as a result of the work done by Samuel Crowther.

The Church Missionary Society sent Crowther on the Niger Expedition of 1854, which had a better outcome. Crowther led the mission consisting entirely of Africans. It was Africans evangelizing Africa. Crowther and J. C. Taylor, an Igbo clergyman from Sierra Leone, joined the next expedition by merchant McGregor Laird to the Niger. Taylor opened an Igbo mission in Onitsha, and Crowther continued up the river and became shipwrecked and stranded for months. While stranded, he studied the Nupe language and looked for openings for mission activity among the Nupe and Hausa peoples. It was the beginning of the Niger Mission. Crowther's Niger mission was significant because it was the first sustained mission among Africa Muslims in modern times. While maintaining Trinitarian doctrine, he established generally cordial relations with Muslim rulers and tried to hear their questions and to correct their misunderstanding of Christianity as polytheistic.

At one point during his ministry, Crowther was arrested by one of the chiefs and held for ransom. The work he was doing was considered a threat to that chief's authority, but English soldiers were able to free Crowther, allowing him to continue his work. Though he often faced threats, his heart for the people around him and his faith in God kept him going. In 1864, Samuel Crowther was appointed the Anglican bishop of Nigeria, making him the first African bishop in the history of the Anglican Church. That same year he was given an honorary Doctorate of Divinity by the University of Oxford. He is remembered as one of the most important Christian figures in the history of the Nigerian church, and his perseverance in the face of opposition and sometimes tangible danger is an example for Christians in every nation.

Mary Slessor

Another important figure in the history of Christianity in Nigeria is Mary Slessor. It is almost impossible to discuss the growth of Christianity in the nation without mentioning one of its great missionaries. Mary Slessor spent much of her life in Nigeria, sharing the gospel through practical demonstrations of the love of Jesus.

Born in Scotland in 1848, Mary had a difficult early life. At the age of eleven, she was forced to begin working in a mill half of the day while

NIGERIA

spending the other half in a school provided by the mill owners. Much of her early life was spent working in the factories of Dundee, Scotland. The education she received gave her the skills of reading and writing, something Mary was thrilled to learn. It was during this time that Mary trusted in Christ as her Savior. She began to help teach a Sunday school class in her church, and she especially loved to share the stories about missionaries and their adventures spreading the gospel around the world.

Mary Slessor, extraordinary missionary to Nigeria, was called the Queen of the Okoyong.

RESTRICTED NATIONS

By age fourteen, Mary was working twelve hours a day in the factory to provide for her family since her father, an alcoholic, had died. It was heartbreaking for her when she had to stop attending school to work more hours, as she loved to learn.

One of the most important things Mary received from her mother was a heart for missions. Each month, Mary's mother received the *Missionary Record*, a publication from the Presbyterian Church in Scotland. This piqued Mary's interest in missions, and she looked forward to receiving the magazine each month. Like many other Scottish youth, her favorite missionary was David Livingstone (1813–1873). Mary could easily identify with Livingstone, as they both were Scottish and had spent their youth working in factories. Livingstone began working in a local cotton mill at age ten and did his school lessons in the evening. He studied medicine and theology in Glasgow and decided to become a missionary doctor. However, he was most known for his exploratory adventures in southern Africa, which he detailed in his bestselling book *Missionary Travels and Researches in South Africa* in 1857.

However, Mary did not believe that she would ever be able to do the things that Livingstone did. Her heart longed to spread God's love to others, but it just did not seem possible because of her family's financial situation. Mary continued to teach in her church, and this experience of shar-

NIGERIA

ing the Good News would prove invaluable to her missionary career.

When she was twenty-seven, Mary Slessor, along with the rest of the world, learned the news of David Livingstone's death on May 1, 1873. He would be honored by being buried in Westminster Abbey. This had a great impact on Mary, who had grown up admiring the courage and faith displayed by Livingstone. It was Livingstone who had said, "I don't care where we go as long as we go forward." His words struck a chord in Mary, and upon his death, she decided she would follow his example and become a missionary. Her mother encouraged her to follow the dream that God had given her.

Amazingly, a little over a year later, Mary Slessor was on the mission field in the Calabar region, modern-day Cross River State in southern Nigeria. The area was rife with tribal superstition, witchcraft, and even the practice of sacrificing children. It truly was a spiritually dark place. With an uncommon determination to spread the gospel, Mary ministered to those around her. Progress was slow, but over time she earned the trust of the people. Unfortunately, Mary became ill with malaria three years into her ministry and was forced to return to Scotland for treatment.

When she recovered, Mary returned to the Calabar region, although this time she moved several miles further inland. Mary adopted a life very similar to the locals, as she sent a large portion of her salary to her mother and sisters back home. This choice led the native Nigerians to more readily accept her because her lifestyle mirrored theirs. Her influence continued to grow steadily in the area.

The worst issue Mary faced in the early years of her ministry was the widespread practice of human sacrifice. This practice was not limited to adults, as many babies were also sacrificed to pagan idols. Twins were considered a curse, and the twins that weren't killed were usually abandoned by their family and left to die. Mary took in all the abandoned children she came across, caring for them and teaching them about Jesus. Her concern for the people and her mastery of the language helped her gain the acceptance of the community. Two deputies from the mission organization were sent to visit Mary and evaluate her progress in the area, and they reported with some surprise that she had earned the friendship and respect of the people she went to serve. It was an impressive feat in an area that had once been quite hostile to missionaries.

In 1888, Mary traveled further north, to an area known as Okoyong. In previous years, the people of that region had responded aggressively toward missionaries, and several were killed. Mary believed that the fact that she was a woman would help the people of the area accept her more easily, and she was right. Mary again earned their trust through her lifestyle and her genuine compassion

NIGERIA

for everyone she met. She would live among the Okoyong for the rest of her life, giving special care to all the orphans who were either brought to her or found abandoned. The Okoyong people respected her opinion so much that she was often called in to settle tribal disputes among the people. She truly was a fixture of the society that she ministered to.

Mary suffered from many deprivations and diseases in her forty years serving in Calabar but she toiled on and left a wonderful legacy of missionary love, concern, and sacrifice. Her work among the people of Calabar was groundbreaking, and when she died of malaria in 1915 she was greatly mourned. The Okoyong people she loved so much affectionately called her the Queen of Okoyong. Mary Slessor spent much of her life spreading the gospel and demonstrating the power of God's love to the people of Calabar. Her work paved the way for other missionaries to enter the area and proved that Nigeria would be a fruitful mission field. To this day she is honored as one of the most important figures in the history of Nigeria. God used her greatly because she was always willing to keep going forward.

RESTRICTED NATIONS

POLITICAL UNREST AND RELIGIOUS VIOLENCE: 2011 POST-ELECTION RIOTS

The road to political and social stability in Nigeria has been a rough one. The pattern of political instability following independence from European colonial powers is evident in Nigeria, and it mirrors the situation in most post-colonial, newly independent countries in Africa. Nigeria's political history is filled with examples of unrest and upheaval, as the different religious and ethnic groups have struggled for control of the country.

From independence in 1960 until 1999, only two governments in Nigeria were produced by a democratic election. Both of those were later overthrown in military coups. Since 1999, Nigeria has moved to a civilian rule. The people have the power to elect their own officials but, unfortunately, fraud and other forms of corruption have marred the results of those elections. Even though Nigeria's electoral process in the first decade of the twenty-first century has not been completely free of corruption, it has been a positive step for the nation. Considering their tumultuous history and present conflicts, it is a noteworthy advancement for a nation struggling to be unified.

Presidential Elections

As 2010 drew toward its conclusion, the nation of Nigeria was busy preparing for its presidential elec-

NIGERIA

tion. From the start, the election seemed doomed to controversy. There was some argument between the political parties over who was running for president. A verbal agreement between the parties declared that the office of president would be filled on a rotation, with a Muslim from the north serving as president for two terms, and then a Christian from the south serving the next two terms. In theory, this would help appease both groups and ensure that both Christians and Muslims would be represented fairly in the government.

The incumbent president, a Christian named Goodluck Jonathan, had come to office after serving as vice president. When the Muslim president he had served under died during his first term, Jonathan completed that term and clearly intended to try to win the election and get another term. His party chose him as their candidate, which upset the Muslim party. It was their opinion that Jonathan should not even run for office, so as to honor the arrangement between the parties. They believed they should have the next term, since Jonathan had come to office only through the death of his Muslim predecessor. To run against Jonathan, they elected Muhammadu Buhari, a Muslim who had the support of most of the northern states. From the start, the election was defined by tension and bickering between the two parties.

The tension was increased when the election was pushed back from the latter part of 2010 into 2011. Nigerian officials were working to implement new voting methods, prompting a delay in the election. This was because previous elections included rampant voter fraud, which government leaders were understandably anxious to limit. The delay had negative consequences, as both campaigns were given more time to stir up controversy and rile up the emotions of their party members. In the months leading up to the election, set for April 2011, several attacks occurred. Some of the attacks were attributed to the extremist group Boko Haram, which was seeking to disrupt the political process and halt the election.

In December 2010, at a political rally in one of Nigeria's southern states, a bomb was detonated, killing several people. In the north, several shootings took place. Both of the candidates publicly declared their disagreement with the attacks, while police and politicians alike blamed the violence on Boko Haram. The attacks certainly did disrupt the elections, but they failed to completely stall them as Boko Haram hoped they would.

Finally, in April 2011, the election took place and, while not completely free of flaws, it was widely praised by Nigerians as being the smoothest and fairest election in the nation's

Goodluck Jonathan, President of Nigeria

history. When the votes were tallied, Goodluck Jonathan, the Christian incumbent, was declared the victor by a wide margin. He had swept the southern states as many expected. It was a different story in the northern states, however. He did not win a majority of the vote in a single northern state. The nation was once again divided, and it would prove to be a significant, ongoing problem, both for the government and for Christians who wish to live in peace.

Post-election Riots and Violence

Only hours after Jonathan was named the winner of the election, rioting broke out in a dozen northern states. Mobs of Islamic supporters shouting "Buhari!" took to the streets, looking for ways to violently express their displeasure with the outcome of the election. They attacked anyone who was known to be a supporter of Jonathan, specifically targeting Christians. Houses that displayed signs supportive of Jonathan were set on fire, and what began as a political riot quickly turned into an assault against Christians. Separating the political and the religious is an impossible task in Nigeria. The Islamic ideology that pervades the Muslim community does not allow for religion and politics to be separate, and it keeps the political as well as religious scenes in constant turmoil.

Early estimates stated that 16,000 people had fled their homes in the north just a couple of days after Jonathan was announced as president. Hundreds of churches were burned and many homes of Christians were destroyed. A mob even destroyed the home of Goodluck Jonathan's running mate, the newly elected vice president Namadi Sambo, a Muslim. Police stations and electoral commission's offices were also targeted by the angry mobs. Christian neighborhoods in the Muslim states were targeted specifically. In some cases, a mob would go door to door, dragging all the Christians from their homes before killing them in the streets. The firsthand accounts of the violence are startling.

One college professor in Kaduna State in northern Nigeria told reporters shortly after the riots that he had witnessed the deaths of five Christians. His account tells of a mob of Muslim youth storming into the school in the middle of the day, chanting the slogan from Buhari's campaign and shouting for Christians to come forward and face them. They had painted their faces and were armed with machetes, clubs, and other weapons. A group of Christians tried to run, but they were chased down and cornered in one of the classrooms. As several tried to escape, three students and a lecturer were killed on the spot, and another student died later of serious wounds in the hospital. The professor said that roughly two hundred additional students were injured by the mob. When the military finally came and got the situation under control, only one person was arrested.

In Kaduna City and the surrounding area, two days of rioting resulted in the deaths of five

NIGERIA

hundred people, while thousands more were displaced after mobs burned homes, businesses, and police stations. In that area alone, three hundred churches were destroyed by fire. Local police forces were ill-equipped and unprepared for the swiftness of the violence. Here, as in many other cases, military forces were needed to finally get the rioting under control. The Voice of the Martyrs provided medical aid, food, and water to the people in the area, though the emergency relief was hardly enough for the thousands of people who were living in camps that the government set up for the refugees.

Unfortunately, some groups of Christians responded to the violence with violence of their own. Many mosques and Muslim homes were also destroyed during the rioting, and there were many Muslim casualties. Muslim leaders stated that a majority of the people killed in Kaduna State were Muslims. They were either attacked by Christians or simply caught up in the violence of the Islamic mobs. For both Muslims and Christians, the violence was horrific. In the twelve northern states where rioting occurred, eight hundred to a thousand people were killed in the three days of rioting. At least another sixty-five thousand people were displaced from their homes following the riots. As one researcher stated, "The April elections were heralded as among the fairest in Nigeria's history, but they were also among the bloodiest."

RESTRICTED NATIONS

In May 2011, President Jonathan appointed a panel to investigate the causes and extent of the election violence. Five hundred people were arrested and charged, though there was little hope at the time that those responsible for the violence would actually face punishment. Many prosecutors fail to follow through due to pressure from their peers, and it is always difficult to know who started the rioting.

The political instability and unrest does not discourage Christians in Nigeria, who know that if they remain faithful they will ultimately receive a more enduring and eternal possession, as Scripture promises: "But recall the former days in which, after you were illuminated, you endured a great struggle with sufferings: partly while you were made a spectacle both by reproaches and tribulations, and partly while you became companions of those who were so treated; for you had compassion on me in my chains, and joyfully accepted the plundering of your goods, knowing that you have a better and an enduring possession for yourselves in heaven" (Hebrews 10:32–34).

NIGERIA

HANDING EVERYTHING TO GOD

Located in the central part of the country, Plateau State is one of the most religiously diverse areas of Nigeria. Having Muslims and Christians living in close proximity has strained relations between the two groups and led to increased violence, turning the state that proclaims itself "The Home of Peace and Tourism" in Nigeria into a place fraught with persecution.

For a young woman named Nvou, the danger that she would be targeted because of her faith was very real. In 2002, militant Muslims seriously injured her husband, and they threatened to return if she did not convert to Islam. It was only weeks later when Nvou, who was seven months pregnant, awoke to the sound of gunshots outside her home. She opened the door to see a mob of armed men surrounding her father-in-law and threatening him, and she quickly slammed the door shut.

The armed men now alerted to her presence, started shouting threats if Nvou did not let them in. They beat on the door angrily and told her that they would burn her house down if she did not open it. Despite their threats, Nvou still did not open the door. The attackers fired a gun twice through the door and then burst in, firing again. This time, Nvou was hit in the hand by a bullet.

RESTRICTED NATIONS

"The second burst of gunfire opened up my abdomen, and my intestines spilled out. I still didn't fall down. When they shot me a third time, breaking my leg, I fell. They then set my house on fire, leaving me to die," Nvou said in later describing the attack to an associate of VOM. Sadly, her two-year-old son was unable to escape and perished in the flames, and the bullet that pierced her abdomen killed her unborn child. She was able to get herself to a local hospital, where she was blessed to learn about Christian doctors who had come to Nigeria to operate on persecuted Christians. The Christian doctors, one of whom was associated with VOMedical, were able to stabilize Nvou's condition and save her life.

"I've handed everything over to God, and I pray He will take care of me," Nvou said during her recovery. "I will continue to work for God; and even if I am killed, it will mean I was killed in the name of the Lord." She continues to display great faith in the midst of her hardships.

NIGERIA

NIGERIA DEALS WITH SHARIAH

Those who know the meaning of Shariah recognize the implications of having to live under such laws. Its repressive stipulations, especially against women, and the manner in which it is enforced on non-Muslims would result in a loss of freedom to be Christian and worship the true God. Nigerian Christians are extremely fearful that Shariah is slowly being imposed on all of Nigeria by radical and violent Muslim groups seeking to make Nigeria an Islamic state. Usually Shariah is implemented in its strictest form and most radical interpretation.

Religion and Politics in Islam

As noted earlier, many Muslims believe that the norm for Islam is to exist within an Islamic state guided by Shariah. In their thinking, Christians and other non-Muslims should be subject to Islamic law because they live in an Islamic land. Politics and religion are part of the total life of submission to Allah and therefore are not separate aspects of life. While the Nigerian Constitution forbids a state religion, radical Muslims see the constitution as a compromise by moderate Muslims to the demands of secularism of the West, so they reject this idea. Those who support the constitution, believing that it is the only way for multiple religious and ethnic groups to live in harmony, see Shariah as the imposition of a state religion on the whole population and believe that Shariah is unconstitutional. The debate is being waged not only in courts; it is also being argued in the streets, and radical groups are trying to force their will on the entire nation through coercion by violence and persecution of religious minorities, particularly Christians.

What Is Shariah?
Shariah is the religious law and moral code based on Islamic traditions. A Muslim would say that Shariah is the divine law of Allah, the way of life prescribed as normative for Muslims by the Islamic prophet Muhammad. It is also the interpretations of the Qur'an by Islamic judges (*quadis*) and religious leaders (*imams*). Much of the law comes directly from the Qur'an and is considered by Muslims to therefore be superior to any other law. As such, Shariah is not subject to any human criticism or alteration, for it is the very thoughts of Allah. Shariah covers many topics addressed by secular laws, like economics, politics, and crime, but also very personal matters such as hygiene, diet, prayer, sex, etiquette, etc. It is a total way of life.

In addition to a strict moral code for things like hygiene and diet, it calls for much harsher punishments for convicted criminals. Under the current system, all citizens in the states with Shariah are subject to Shariah, whether they are Muslim or not. Human rights concerns have been raised over the harsh punishments that some

NIGERIA

states are now legally allowed to hand out. Convicted adulterers are sentenced to death by stoning, and thieves are to be punished by having a hand cut off. In 2002, a woman in Sokoto State was accused of adultery and sentenced to death by stoning, the proper punishment according to Shariah. The woman claimed throughout the trial that she was raped, but she was still convicted because Shariah requires four male witnesses to corroborate the claim of a woman. Only three men testified in her favor during her case. Her story was picked up by international media, and the outrage that arose over her trial eventually got her pardoned. This is just one example of the harshness of Shariah, which is viewed by experts as being much stricter on women than on men. Christians in the country fear that they are slowly being relegated to "second-class" status and that the nation as a whole is moving toward becoming a total Muslim state. This is referred to by experts as the "Islamization" of the country.

Shariah and the Establishment of Political Order

Shariah has been an important and controversial topic in Nigeria since the 1970s. As the Nigerian Constitution was being drafted in 1978, Muslims in the north lobbied for a Shariah court of appeals. Once the constitution was completed and ratified, Shariah was no longer on the forefront of the nation's consciousness, at least for a while. It was not until 1999 that Shariah would once again become a hot-button issue.

Shariah has been used in the predominantly Muslim north long before the colonial administration of Nigeria came into being. It has recently become politicized when the state of Zamfara, then eleven other states, decided to adopt Shariah. Local Christians were upset, fearing that the changes would negatively impact how they would be treated. Despite the protests and controversy surrounding the decision, Zamfara did adopt what Paul Marshall of the Hudson Institute described as "a draconian version of Shariah." In reality, Shariah presents a direct challenge to the authority of the federal government, substituting Shariah law for national laws that take all religions into consideration. It is the imposition of Islamic laws on non-Muslims. Taxes paid by citizens of all religions go to pay for Islamic preachers, while many churches are being closed.

Some of the most disturbing aspects of Shariah pertain to women and how they rate in Islamic society. Shariah allows a man to marry a girl as young as nine years of age. While a man is allowed four wives, a woman can have only one husband. Muslim men can divorce their wives at any time for any reason, but a woman needs the consent of her husband to seek a divorce. Shockingly, Shariah allows a husband to beat his wife for anything that he deems as insubordination. Women are allowed to testify only in property cases, and even

NIGERIA

then their testimony carries only half the weight of a man's. Under Shariah, a woman who has been raped is not even allowed to testify against her attackers, and it requires that four male witnesses corroborate a woman's testimony of rape. Also, women are not permitted to drive cars, and any woman who is seen speaking alone to a man she is not related to is breaking Shariah law and must be severely punished. Women are treated as second-class citizens at best, and as property at worst.

Christians fear living in a society where they would be subjugated to Shariah, because they would not have as many rights in a Shariah court as they have in the state or democratic courts.

Christians Oppose Imposition of Shariah

Shortly after the announcement about Shariah being adopted by Zamfara State on January 27, 2000, Christians in Kaduna City, Nigeria, found themselves in a difficult situation. Kaduna City had a very large population of Christians, and they considered Shariah rule to be an attack on their freedoms. Kaduna City experienced some of the most brutal religious riots in Nigeria's history, and they can be directly traced to the decision to implement Shariah. Officials estimate that two thousand died, although there is not a precise count of those killed, maimed, or wounded in the riots. Over two hundred churches were burned down, as well as over one hundred mosques. Close to nine thousand homes were destroyed, displacing thousands, and many children lost one or both of their parents.

In February 2000, fifty thousand Christians gathered to stage a peaceful demonstration against Shariah in Kaduna City. They moved throughout the city, eventually going to the Government House, where the governor resides, hoping to present their case to the state's decision makers. Minutes before the leaders of the Christian procession were to have their appeal heard by the governor, a rumor spread among the gathered believers that another Christian in the city had just been killed by Muslims. Tensions were already high, and the rumor was more than enough to set off a new wave of religious violence.

Observers would later note that the pattern of violence was replicated throughout Kaduna. The mobs would typically start by going to the churches, killing the pastor and burning the church, and then the violence spread to other parts of the city. This resulted in the deaths of hundreds of Christians who were hiding in their churches and the destruction of a tremendous amount of Christian property. When the president of Nigeria visited Kaduna after the February riots, he found the city "in ruins."

The Effects of the Kaduna Riots

A Nigerian writer described the Kaduna riots as "one of the darkest episodes in the history of religious conflicts in this country. The destruction

NIGERIA

was horrendous, as was the senselessness of the rampage." President Olusegun Obasanjo, a Christian who served as a military officer in the Nigerian Civil War and had seen many battlefields, is quoted after seeing the city: "I could not believe that Nigerians were capable of such barbarism against one another." The city looked like a battlefield, with bodies strewn along the streets and buildings burned.

Shariah continues to cause the persecution of Christians and to create an atmosphere for violence and conflict. Extremist Muslim groups, such as Boko Haram, want the entire country to be governed by Shariah, and they seek to drive out or kill Christians in order to establish it. Christians are keenly aware of their precarious situation and many are willing to witness to their Muslim neighbors, realizing that such faithfulness could be costly in this life but will be rewarded in the next. Many Christians also realize that physical violence is not the answer to injustice. Rose, who lost her pastor husband in a 2001 religious riot in Kaduna, acknowledges, "There is power in the name of Jesus. I don't know how it is in America, but in Nigeria we need the power of that name when we pray." Rose takes care of other Christian widows in her area, supporting them in any way she can. As Paul says in 1 Corinthians 16:13,14: "Watch, stand fast in the faith, be brave, be strong. Let all that you do be done with love."

TESTIMONY: RESPONDING LIKE JESUS

Dahiru had a privileged youth. The eldest son of a clan chief in Plateau State, he was raised with the anticipation that he would one day be chief, which meant great prestige and honor in society, especially among Muslims. He joined the Muslim Brotherhood, a militant extremist force dedicated to seeing Nigeria became a fully Islamic state. His membership in the organization allowed him to be sent to Saudi Arabia and Sudan for six months of training. The Muslim Brotherhood is not a political party but is a movement that interprets Islam conservatively and works to implement Shariah as the basis for controlling the affairs of society and the state. It also seeks to unify all Islamic countries and to liberate them from foreign influence and power, and to reclaim the Islamic empire that once stretched from Spain to Indonesia.

Upon his return, Dahiru was involved in planning and carrying out attacks and other violent acts against Christians in the area. He traveled all over Nigeria, zealously engaging in *jihad*, willing to fight and die to rid Nigeria of Christians.

However, God had other plans for Dahiru. God began to soften his heart and eventually Dahiru turned to the Lord and became a Christian. He left the Muslim Brotherhood, which meant giving up his prestige among his peers, choosing instead

NIGERIA

to live his life for his newfound Savior. Like the apostle Paul, he found himself a member of the very group that he had tried so hard to destroy.

The members of Dahiru's clan no longer respect him. He is no longer met with gazes of awe and honor that he once received as a respected member of the Brotherhood. Instead of accolades, he is now the recipient of hatred, spite, and rejection from his family and friends.

In 2001, he witnessed the brutality of Islamic *jihad*, as the city of Jos was attacked by radical Muslims. Christians were targeted and killed, and in many cases the tactics used were the same ones that Dahiru had learned and utilized in his former lifestyle. When he saw the suffering of his fellow Christians, Dahiru struggled. How should he respond to these atrocities? It would be easy and natural to respond with hatred and retaliation, making the attackers suffer for what they had done. However, Dahiru quickly realized that this was not the response Jesus would want and he was reminded by his pastor that when Jesus was persecuted during His time on earth, He never raised a hand against His attackers. Though He was hated, He responded with love. Dahiru gave up his hate and forgave the people who carried out the attack. It became evident that the transformation in his life had been real and was an incredible example of the redeeming work of Christ.

BAD MEAT, BAD BLOOD

It doesn't take much to start a riot in parts of Nigeria. Consider the Bauchi riots of 1991. The circumstances that actually sparked the violence are unclear, but unfortunately, it takes only a spark for the religious tensions between the extremely devoted Muslims and their Christian neighbors to ignite into outright violence.

The starting point for the riots in Bauchi State was the village of Tafawa Balewa. Among the various accounts of the incident that began the riot, the most widely accepted story is that a Christian butcher was being confronted by a Muslim customer, who angrily claimed that the butcher had sold him meat that was unacceptable for him to eat due to his Islamic beliefs. The argument got so heated that the Muslim unsheathed a knife and slashed the arm of the butcher.

Several of the butcher's Christian friends heard the confrontation and rushed to his aid after he shouted in pain. They tried to calm the situation down, but they were soon overwhelmed by a mob of Muslims who had come to assist their Muslim brother. The mob beat up the Christians, and the incident led to a citywide riot that lasted four days. After they left the butcher's shop, the religious fervor of the Muslim group grew. They marched throughout the town, burning the homes of Christians, as well as hotels and churches.

NIGERIA

In the four days it took for the authorities to bring the situation under control, thousands of Christians had fled the village, fearing for their lives. Most of them went to neighboring states, hoping that they would be safe there. In those few days, two hundred people were killed, hundreds more were injured in the chaos, and twenty churches were burned to the ground.

The riot set off a new wave of attacks across much of Bauchi State impacting many of the villages surrounding Tafawa Balewa, and eventually even the capital of the state, Bauchi City. As crowds of Muslims in Bauchi City took to the streets, bent on eliminating Christianity from the area, the homes and businesses of known Christians were targeted and attacked, and another twenty church buildings were destroyed. In just three days, five hundred homes were set on fire and badly damaged and five hundred people were killed. While it cannot be said with certainty that the dead were all Christians, since the mobs were uncontrolled and non-Christians may have fallen victim to the violence, it is certain that Christians were the targets of the violence across Bauchi City.

One man later told a Nigerian reporter. that he witnessed his brother, Johnson, being burned alive by the mob. Johnson was a Christian who was in his shop when the mob set the building ablaze. He tried to get out, but several members of the group stopped him and forced him back inside. One man threatened him with a long blade,

RESTRICTED NATIONS

and others used long sticks to shove him back into the burning building. Eventually the structural integrity of the building failed, and Johnson was killed when the roof collapsed on him.

All told, the violence in Bauchi State in 1991 claimed the lives of one thousand people, with a great percentage of those being Christians who were specifically targeted for their faith. Religious tensions in the area were so high that a simple misunderstanding at a butcher shop led to what would become one of the most violent riots in Nigerian history. This is just one example of the environment that is created by the close proximity of these two opposing beliefs. Yakubu Joseph and Rainer Rothfuss, writing on the problem of segregating religious communities in the Middle Belt of Nigeria, say that the main problems that plague the Plateau State (southwest of Bauchi State) are endemic religious intolerance and the struggle to reintroduce historic Islamic domination through religious extremism. This sets up a volatile situation that needs little for it to explode into a full-fledged riot.

In parts of Nigeria Christians must face a life complicated by the potential for unexpected and often unprovoked violence. Yet, they continue to serve the Lord and keep the faith, knowing that their present circumstances in no way compare to the glory to come as they remain faithful. That doesn't make their situation less volatile, but it makes it far more bearable since they know God has His purposes for the difficult times.

NIGERIA

PROSTHETIC LIMBS FOR PERSECUTED CHRISTIANS

During many brutal attacks, machetes wielded by extremist Muslims have cut off arms and legs, leaving Christians unable to work and provide for their families. Some have lost a limb in an explosion and saw their ability to care for their loved ones taken away in one cruel blast. These injuries are some of the most devastating for Christians in Nigeria. In addition to the physical pain, they also face the prospect of being without an arm or a leg for the rest of their life. Who will provide for their family if they are unable to? Most of these men and women have jobs that require physical labor, and their wounds limit their ability to do their work.

For years, VOMedical has provided care to Christians who suffered injuries from their persecutors. They have been a great blessing to the persecuted church in Nigeria, and in 2013 a new opportunity for care arose for these Christians. In that year, a team of American doctors visited Nigeria to volunteer with VOMedical and other groups that provide medical aid to the persecuted. This team specialized in the making and fitting of prosthetic limbs, and they were able to create custom prostheses for many Christians who were facing this crisis. They were also able to train local medical staff and VOMedical workers stationed in Nigeria in the construction of the limbs, so that the prosthetics clinic could function even after they returned to the States.

The clinic saw immediate and dramatic results.

- John, who lost his job as a driver because he couldn't drive a manual vehicle with only one leg, received a new prosthetic leg.
- Rachel, the sole provider for her five children, can once again stand in the garden to cultivate the vegetation.
- When Weng Goodluck Tshua was an infant, men attacked his home, throwing him and his mother into the fire that destroyed his home. His mother was killed, but Weng was rescued. Although he survived the attack, the flames badly damaged both of his legs and he was crippled from his injuries. As he grew older, the damage worsened, and he couldn't even crawl. At four years old, Weng has been in the care of VOMedical for years, but it became increasingly difficult for him to walk. It wasn't until the establishment of this prosthetics clinic that Weng had any prospect of ever being able to walk again. The possibility of being fitted for prosthetics gives Weng hope that he will one day be able to walk and play with the other little boys in his village.

Innocent Bystander: Vincent Godwin's Story
Trying to live a normal life allowed one Christian to become a target for religious hatred and violence.

NIGERIA

A nice evening in April 2011 turned into a nightmare for twenty-four-year-old Vincent Godwin who was on his way to the grocery store to pick up some needed items. He was stopped by a mob of angry Muslim men, many of whom Godwin recognized instantly; they were his neighbors in Kaduna City.

Unfortunately, the men cared little that Godwin was a neighbor. Enraged by the result of the national presidential election, they surrounded Godwin because they knew he was a Christian, and at that moment they hated him for it. Several of the men were armed with machetes, and they began to attack him with their sharpened blades.

Desperate to defend himself, Godwin raised his arms to protect his face. The blade savagely cut through one arm, severing it from his body. Pleased with themselves the mob left quickly, eager to take out their rage on others. They must have thought that Godwin would bleed to death so they left him to die.

Somehow, Godwin remained conscious after the assault, and he had the presence of mind to pick up his severed limb and rushed to a nearby military hospital. Doctors there were unable to save his arm, although they were able to close the wound and save Godwin's life.

A short time after Godwin lost his arm, the VOMedical workers were able to fit him with a prosthesis, which Godwin adjusted to quickly.

RESTRICTED NATIONS

The beauty of the story is that Godwin has forgiven those who attacked him, displaying a grace that can only come from God. God will reward those who display such a spirit. Matthew writes: "Blessed are you when they revile and persecute you, and say all kinds of evil against you falsely for My sake. Rejoice and be exceedingly glad, for great is your reward in heaven, for so they perse-

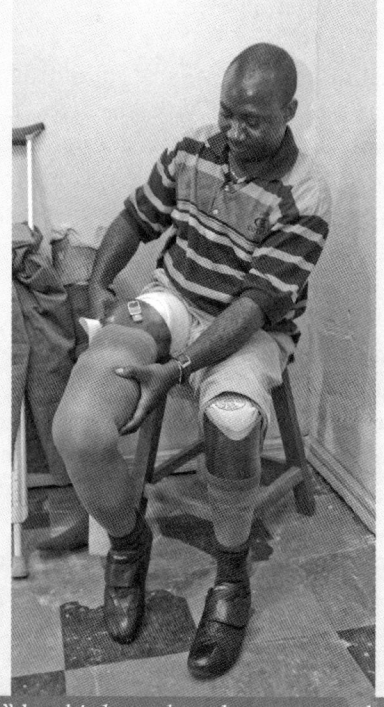

"Monte" lost his legs when they were crushed by a vehicle in an attack on a Christian neighborhood.

72

NIGERIA

cuted the prophets who were before you" (Matthew 5:11,12).

A Clinic: A Place for Healing

The clinic is unique, the first of its kind in Nigeria. The lab continues to create new limbs, which are offered freely to persecuted Christians in the area as a practical display of the love of Christ and the unity of the worldwide church.

"While the bodies of our brothers and sisters in Nigeria may have been broken, the condition of their faith is tremendously strong," wrote one VOM worker who spent time at the new facility. The Christians who are receiving these new limbs are being given an opportunity to continue their lives as normal. They are able to demonstrate the love of Christ to their communities. As one of the prosthetics practitioners shared with several of his patients, "Now you can walk and be living evidence of Christ's love to your Muslim persecutors!"

The faith of these Nigerian Christians continues to encourage us. One VOMedical volunteer wrote about her experience in Nigeria and her time at the clinic, saying, "The prosthetic limbs...will enable them to walk, but it has always been the Nigerian believers' abundance of grace and forgiveness amid persecution that truly allows them to heal."

BOKO HARAM, ANSARU, AND FULANI HERDSMEN: PRESENT-DAY PERSECUTORS

Nigeria is one of the greatest "Islamo-Christian" nations in the world. Muib O. Opeloy, who teaches religion in Nigeria, has coined this term to help explain Nigeria's Muslim and Christian interactions. As already noted, Nigeria has large populations of Muslims and Christians living side by side, with the north predominantly Muslim and the south predominantly Christian, each living alongside animistic religions. Both Islam and Christianity are represented by large populations in states dominated by the other religion.

The tension between the north and the south is fueled, many believe, by a number of issues—economic, political, and religious. The situation is not so simplistic that one can say religion is the only cause of the conflict, but it is one of the leading factors and at times seems to be the prominent motivation behind the violence against and persecution of Christians in the country. It is clear, however, that the real issue driving the extremist groups is religion. Some have explicitly stated that their main goal is to return Nigeria to an Islamic state and adopt Shariah for the whole country, exterminating Christians and even Muslims who do not follow their extremist teachings. The primary threat to Christians is from the Boko Haram, Ansaru, and Fulani herdsmen.

NIGERIA

Nigeria has had a long and unfortunate history of conflicts between various communities and ethno-religious groups that have led to riots claiming the lives of thousands. The social situation in northern Nigeria is in many ways deplorable, with the worst maternal and infant mortality rates in the world. It is also estimated that Nigeria has over 700,000 people in slavery. The Global Slavery Index defines slavery as persons who are denied freedom because they are possessed or controlled by others and are exploited for profit or sex, and this includes forced marriage, the kidnapping of children to serve in war, or indentured servitude. Child marriage in Nigeria is still commonplace.

Boko Haram
One of the extremist groups that has sprung up in the last decade in Nigeria and has grown especially notorious for violent attacks is Boko Haram. It is a terrorist organization with links to al-Qaeda. The term *Boko Haram*, which roughly translates to "Western education is sin" in the Hausa language, is really a term of derision. One of its aims is to destroy modern education because it was begun in Nigeria by Christians and was used, they think, to make converts of Muslims. In 2002 a radical youth group formed in the Alhaji Muhammadu Ndimi Mosque in Maiduguri, and Boko Haram is an offshoot of this youth group. It declared that it was going on a *hijra* (the journey of

the Prophet Mohammad and his followers from Mecca to Medina when Mohammad's life was threatened) and then its members would withdraw, as the Prophet Mohammad withdrew from Mecca to Medina. They moved to the village of Kanama in the Yobe State to form a separatist community that reflected hardline Islamic principles.

The earliest leader was Mohammad Ali, who sought to live under true Islamic law, creating a more perfect society away from the corrupt society of Nigeria, including even the Muslim government which they felt was unredeemable. In 2003 Ali was killed in a battle with police during a siege of their mosque to recover weapons stolen earlier from officers.

Return to Maiduguri and the Leadership of Mohammed Yusuf

The survivors of the group later returned to Maiduguri and formed again under the leadership of Mohammed Yusuf, who desired to establish a new mosque. They located on a large farm owned by Yusuf's father-in-law, and their goal was to create a state within a state, a government parallel to the federal government, with its own cabinet and religious police. In 2007 Sheikh Ha'afar Mahmound Ada, a regular preacher at the Nmidi Mosque in Maiduguri and a prominent cleric in the community, was assassinated while praying in a mosque in Kano. His murder remained a mystery for a long time but it is now thought that he was killed because he had criticized the Boko Haram for their hardline ideology. He predicted that they would clash with the state. His assassination was a key point in the development of the radical aspect of Boko Haram, because from that point on there was no possibility of getting Yusuf and his followers to rejoin the mainstream of the northern Islamic establishment. John Campbell, former US ambassador to Nigeria, describes Boko Haram as a kind of personality cult, as well as an Islamic sect that dreamed of the religion's revival and a new golden age of Islam.

It is important to know more about Mohammed Yusuf. Boko Haram is described by one author as the most violent of the extremist groups currently active in Nigeria. They focus primarily on Nigeria, while another group, the Ansaru—an offshoot of Boko Haram founded by Mohammed Yusuf—focuses more on foreigners and foreign interests. Their extremism moves beyond just setting up an ideal Islamic kingdom in Nigeria, but seeks to destroy anything and anyone who might stand in the way of a global dominance of radical Islam.

Yusuf's formation as an extremist began in his youth when he became enamored with the leading Islamist currents of his day. One of the groups was Ibrahim al-Zakzaky's Islamic Movement of Nigeria (IMN), funded by Iran. The IMN drew its inspiration from the Egyptian Muslim

Brotherhood, which had revived the concept of an Islamic state governed by Shariah. Al-Zakzaky and other Sunnis (the larger of two major divisions of Islam) broke away from the IMN when they determined that the IMN had a Shi'a (the smaller division of Islam) agenda, including the veneration of Iranian leaders and the observance of Shi'a religious rights.

The Salafi Movement
Yusuf later came to believe that Muslims should follow true Salafists and that all others were infidels. The Salafi movement within Sunni Islam was an attempt to return to their predecessors' ways, which came to be known as a literalist, strict, and puritanical approach to Islam. It surfaced in the second half of the nineteenth century in reaction to the spread of European ideas. Yusuf joined the Salafist group referred to as JTI (Jamiat Talaba-e-Islam), which was a movement for the revival of Islam. Later the JTI became incorporated by the Izala movement (Movement or Society for the Removal of Innovation and Reestablishment of Sunni Islam) and Yusuf affiliated with them. He studied under the Saudi-trained imam Sheikh Jafa'ar Adam, but later challenged him in sermons about Salafi doctrine. He became the Borno representative on Sheikh Datti Ahmed's Supreme Council for Shariah in Nigeria, which sought to Islamicize Nigeria. Becoming dissatisfied with the implementation of Shariah in Nigeria, Ahmed and

NIGERIA

other members of the Supreme Council formed a new movement called Companions of the Prophet. They became known as the Nigerian Taliban.

Yusuf believed that Western institutions were corrupting Muslims. He thought that every Christian teaching regarding God and the universe was fundamentally and totally different from Islamic revelation. He cited the work of a Saudi Wahhabist (an ultraconservative sect within Sunni Islam) scholar, Bakr bin Abdullan Abut Zyad, who taught that European colonists introduced secular Western education into Islamic society as a means of controlling them and corrupting Islamic morals.

Yusuf longed for the past glory of the Borno State, his birthplace, which once was the home of an ethnic Kanuri-led Islamic Caliphate that lasted from about AD 1000 to the end of the nineteenth century. Yusuf was ethnic Kanuri and his message resonated with fellow Kanuris. They were the first ethnic group to fully embrace Islam, while the ethnic Fulani and Hausa Muslims, because they were tied closely to the Nigerian government, had rejected true Islam for secularism and democracy. Yusuf believed the present government was merely a carryover of the old colonial system and that the leaders were secularized Muslims who perpetuated the Western dominance over Muslims. He pinned the blame for all the economic, political, and social troubles on them. Yusuf had no faith in the Nigerian government as it was and felt that it and the Muslim ruling class in Nigeria needed to

RESTRICTED NATIONS

be swept away and replaced with a new government composed of Salafists. In the early 2000s he sent some of his followers abroad to Algeria and Mauritania for jihadist training through the AQIM (Al-Qaeda in the Islamic Maghreb), revealing that he had wider associations than just in Nigeria, but also associated with the broader radical Islamic groups like Al-Qaeda.

Source of Boko Haram's Radical Ideas

Initially the main desire of Boko Haram was to withdraw from society, which they saw as corrupt and non-Muslim (at least as they interpret it). They drew radical ideas from the thirteenth-century Muslim scholar Ibn Taymiyyah, who was also cited by Salafist radicals. It is anti-European and seeks to expose the modern roots of Muslim civilization and society. Boko Haram and the Salafists share much ideology in common. Radical Salafi jihadists believe *jihad* against civilians is a correct expression of Islam, even though Salafi scholars condemn the attacks. They also desire to impose Shariah over all of Nigeria. This goes hand-in-hand with the restoration of purely Islamic education as they conceive of it. They are completely opposed to any belief or way of life that is not based in strict, traditional Islamic teaching. They wish to purify the Tsangaya system of schools where clerics teach students to memorize the Qur'an. Often it is the poor who attend these schools since they cannot afford to attend modern

(Western-style) schools. Students beg during the day and give the money to their teachers when they begin their studies in the evening. These young men have a fervent Muslim belief system, but they lack practical life skills with which to earn a living. In many cases, these youths join groups like Boko Haram, which appeal to their religious zeal and promise them a chance to serve Allah. This has been noted by Nigerian experts as a very real issue in the more highly Muslim areas of the country.

Critics of Boko Haram point out that Islam has a broad tradition of education, not limited to the narrow view of radical groups like Boko Haram. Their concept of education, according to Muib Opeloye, is grossly un-Islamic and hypocritical. And, despite being against Western education, Boko Haram uses modern technology and other means that have been developed in the West to further their cause.

Desire to Become Nigerian Taliban
Toward the end of first decade of the twenty-first century, Yusuf looked more and more toward the Taliban in Afghanistan, al-Qaeda, and Osama bin Laden as models for Nigerian *jihad*. He forbade his followers to participate in sports since it would mean association with non-Muslims, which is against the Salafist principle of not developing affection for non-Muslims. Yusuf had a strong admiration for Algerian Islamists, and the effect of their views on his beliefs and actions cannot be

overestimated. On one occasion Yusuf heard the Algerians pronounce a *fatwâ* (an Islamic religious ruling) that prohibited Muslim militants from attending school or working for governments, and he applied it wholesale to Nigeria. Yusuf believed that the Islamization of the Nigerian government should be done through preaching, preferring spiritual persuasion rather than the use of violence. But in the end, he believed that violent *jihad* was the solution for Nigerian Muslims, and he was willing to use violence when required.

Under Yusuf's leadership, Boko Haram launched violent attacks across the country. His forces targeted the city of Maiduguri in 2009, attacking churches and Christian homes, as well as government buildings such as police stations, prisons, and schools. The city was devastated by the ferocity of the assault. The riots spread to other states, and Boko Haram destroyed nearly everything in its path for five days before police were finally able to get the situation under control.

Christians were targeted specifically, as witnesses report seeing Christians taken from their homes and forced under the threat of death to renounce their faith in Christ. Many Christians bravely clung to their faith, ultimately giving up their lives. Seven hundred were reported dead in the city of Maiduguri alone after the attack was over. In July 2009, shortly before his death, Yusuf declared that his militia would "hunt and gun down those who oppose the rule of Shariah in Nigeria

NIGERIA

and ensure that the infidel does not go unpunished." There is little question, then, that Boko Haram is fighting a war of religion. Boko Haram has continued to operate in Nigeria, emboldened by Yusuf's sacrifice of his life for the cause.

Yusuf's Hypocrisy

Yusuf, however, did not entirely practice what he preached. According to *Newswatch* (August 10, 2009), he drove expensive exotic cars, sent his children to private schools where they received a quality education, and had a bevy of private lawyers and doctors to attend to him and his family, while at the same time he preached and advocated against these very things to his followers. He tried to escape capture by the Nigerian army by going to his father-in-law's home in neighboring Chad, but was found hiding in a chicken coop and arrested. He was turned over to the police and subsequently reported as having died.

The Boko Haram that has emerged in recent years appears to have an allegiance to radical Islamic groups from other Muslim countries, including al-Qaeda. Boko Haram receives training and supplies from some of these groups, using them against the people of Nigeria. Just one month after Yusuf was killed by Nigerian military forces, the group's leaders released a statement that declared loyalty to al-Qaeda, and issued a call to Muslims to take part in *jihad* in Nigeria. Since this call to action, Boko Haram has been populated by Muslims from places like Mali, Mauritania, and Algeria.

The group is gaining more favor with the radical Islamic movement. Several reports state that some members of Boko Haram have been seen at known al-Qaeda training facilities. The group now has outside support from one of the most dangerous terrorist organizations in the world. In fact, some experts believe that Boko Haram is currently the second most dangerous terrorist network in the world, behind only the Taliban, despite the fact that it is operating in only one country. Interestingly, no al-Qaeda affiliate has recognized Boko Haram as one of their own. Their level of random violence may even be such that it would tarnish the image of al-Qaeda.

Another Return to Maiduguri
In 2010, Boko Haram returned to Maiduguri and started a campaign of assassinations. This is when many believe that Boko Haram began having connections with foreign and international terrorist organizations, although their focus is on Nigeria. They have since broadened their targets to other representations of authority.

Some argue that it is difficult to pin down exactly who Boko Haram is since they returned to Maiduguri. Their acts and targets of terror seem random, and their tactics continue to evolve since they are very adaptive. The organization is a loosely connected cell-like structure with many factions and splits. There is reportedly a thirty-member Shura Council that superintends the many cells of Boko Haram, with each cell being responsible for a different geographical area.

Little about the organization can be verified and dependable information is hard to come by. Abdul Raufu Mustapha, a Nigerian who teaches African politics at the Department of International Development at the University of Oxford, says there are a number of motives attributed to Boko Haram, and there are conspiracy theories as well. Their mystique adds to their threat. What can be truly said is that they are an Islamo-political terrorist group that uses religion to manipulate the political situation.

Some have called Boko Haram thugs and anti-socials. It is possible that criminal elements have acted under the banner of Boko Haram with their primary purpose to commit crimes rather than change the political horizon. The goal of Boko Haram, however, remains to impose their ideology on every Nigerian and their dominion over all of Nigeria. They want to create a "closed totalitarian theocracy." More specifically, they want to create a pure Islamic state ruled by Shariah. Their random and indiscriminate attacks have the potential of losing the support of their host communities. More Muslims, it is reported, have been killed by Boko Haram than Christians. It is an ugly and bloody war against the nation.

RESTRICTED NATIONS

Christian Targets

Christians remain the focus of much of the Boko Haram's anger. In recent years the group has chosen Christian holidays as the setting for attacks. In 2011, Boko Haram detonated a bomb that targeted Christians leaving St. Theresa Catholic Church after Christmas morning mass. The blast happened in a suburb of Nigeria's capital of Abuja, and many were killed and the church completely destroyed. Only a crater was left. Other churches were targeted as well and more than eighty-five people died that day due to terrorist actions. It was the second consecutive year that Boko Haram had attacked Christians as they were celebrating the birth of Christ.

A week later, on January 1, 2012, Boko Haram issued a warning to all Christians in northern Ni-

A church building burned by radical Muslims in 2010 shows the devastation to churches in Nigeria.

NIGERIA

geria that they had three days to leave the area. If they did not comply, the attacks would increase. Viciously true to their word, Boko Haram killed half as many people in January 2012 as they did the whole year prior. In a video posted on the Internet on January 11, Boko Haram declared war on Christians in Nigeria.

On Easter morning in 2012, Boko Haram used a suicide car bomber to attack a Protestant church in Kaduna State. Thirty-nine were killed and dozens more wounded. They do these horrific crimes seemingly without remorse or regret.

The church in Nigeria has been forced to respond to Boko Haram's terrorist activity. Many congregations post uniformed armed guards outside the church building, patrolling the perimeter in case of attack. A VOM worker who visited the country saw one congregation that completely closes the road around the church grounds, fearful of someone using a car bomb. Everyone must park in the road, away from the building. The violence aimed at them has made many congregations take such precautions. They have also responded spiritually by calling Christians to times of fasting and prayer. Despite this great persecution, the church in Nigeria continues to be effective and vibrant. God continues to move in the land in the midst of the hostility.

Since the early 2000s, Boko Haram has killed thousands of Nigerians and driven countless more from their communities. Boko Haram has become one of the most dangerous threats in Nigeria, both to religious freedom and democracy. There has been a call to hold a Sovereign National Conference to try to resolve the country's issues and restore unity because many believe the country is on the brink of falling over a precipice to chaos and dysfunction.

Boko Haram poses a real threat to the unity, peace, and stability of the country of Nigeria. True federalism, remarks one scholar, means fostering peaceful coexistence among the many religious and ethnic groups in the country. Boko Haram is considered by many to be murderers and terrorists who justify their evil by an appeal to religion. Theirs is a shadowy campaign of terror to purify Nigeria from Western values and to rid the nation of democracy.

Nigeria has taken steps to combat groups such as Boko Haram. In October 2013, Boko Haram attacked the small town of Benisheik, dragging men from their homes and killing them in the streets. Motorists were stopped by armed gunmen and shot while still in their vehicles. It took ten hours for the Nigerian military to mount a response, and in that time, at least one hundred and fifty people were killed.

However, in nearby Maiduguri, Boko Haram has been repelled by a group of civilian vigilantes. The city was attacked by Yusuf and his forces in 2009, and since then has been repeatedly terrorized by Boko Haram. Thousands of civilians fled the city out of fear, but they are now returning because of the success of the vigilante force. This force, which has been encouraged and even funded by the governor of the state, Governor Shettima, is composed of civilians and is far more effective at stopping the agents of Boko Haram than the military has been. They know everyone in the community and are able to turn in any suspicious characters before violence breaks out. The success of the vigilante force, which calls itself the Civilian Joint Task Force, has led some of Nigeria's officials to consider training other civilian groups to work against Boko Haram.

Some within the country speculate that the military's ineffectiveness is due to the use of standard military methods, whereas fighting against an insurgency requires different tactics of engaging in warfare. Nearly a quarter of the Nigerian government's budget is spent on national security, but this money has done little to stop Boko Haram from rampaging across northern Nigeria.

New Boko Haram Leader
Yusuf's death at the hands of security forces, in what has become known as an "extrajudicial killing," led to the transition of power in Boko Haram to a more violent and militant leader named Abubakar Shekau, who served as a deputy to Yusuf. Some in Boko Haram believe that Shekau had ordered the violence against the police, which backfired and led to Yusuf's death, so they joined

Ansaru instead of following Shekau. While Yusuf spoke of *jihad* primarily in ideological terms, Shekau sought to implement violent *jihad* by igniting confrontation. Shekau had many radical ideas similar to Yusuf. He was strongly anti-Western and more specifically anti-American. He believed that Christians are in fact enemies of Boko Haram and should be eliminated from Nigeria, and that Western education is the root of evil in the world and must be replaced by religious (Muslim) education. Christians are polytheists and Judeo-Christian tradition has fostered the practice of more liberal interpretations of religious texts in most modern religions and therefore has had a corrupting influence on Islam, particularly on Muslims trained in the West. Consequently, a true Muslim will have no association with Christians.

Yusuf had taught that Europeans incorrectly believe that religion is separate from politics, and

The current leader of Boko Haram in Nigeria, Abubakar Shekau

that religion is purely a private affair that should be eliminated from the public domain and debate. Shekau echoed many of Yusuf's sentiments. Democracy, Shekau believes, is seen as a rejection of God's sovereign and supreme leadership over creation. A multiparty democracy, as well as a constitution affirming the secular identity of the present regime, is an offense to the sovereignty and rule of God alone. Abubakar Shekau has publicly stated his goal for Nigeria: "Everyone knows that democracy and the constitution is paganism. You Christians should know that Jesus...is not the son of God. This religion of Christianity you are practicing is not a religion of God—it is paganism. We are trying to coerce you to embrace Islam, because that is what [Allah] instructed us to do." Shekau desires to change the political system by introducing God's law, Shariah, to destroy democracy and the constitution, which he believes are forbidden themes in Islam.

The Terrorism Continues
In the last few years Boko Haram has become especially cruel and brazen in their attacks. In July 2012 armed terrorists went on a twelve-village killing spree in Nigeria's Plateau State murdering over one hundred people. Boko Haram has taken responsibility for the massacre. The group allegedly attacked and killed twenty-five to thirty Christian students at a university in northeastern Nigeria on October 1, 2012. In the late night hours

masked gunmen went into an off-campus housing section of Federal Polytechnic College of Mubi and went door-to-door, separating the Muslim students from the Christians, and then shooting or slitting the throats of the Christian students. In a September 2013 attack Boko Haram seemed to randomly target residents of Nigeria's Borno State, killing about a hundred and sixty people. On September 29, 2013, it is suspected that Islamic extremists gunned down dozens of students at Yobe State College of Agriculture in Gujba as they slept in their dormitories during a nighttime attack. As many as fifty students may have been killed in the assault.

In February 2014 Boko Haram attacked a remote boarding school also in the Yobe State, killing twenty-nine teenage boys, five of whom were reportedly Christians. Before the attack they had gathered the female students and told them to stop studying, and go home and get married. In

A Nigerian widow portrays the resilience and peace of Christ in spite of her losses.

NIGERIA

April a bomb exploded in a bus station in Abuja, Nigeria's federal capital, killing seventy-one people and injuring over a hundred and twenty. News reports said that "suspicion fell on Boko Haram" although they had not yet claimed responsibility for the attack. It appeared to fit their pattern of soft civilian targets in seemingly random attacks.

Boko Haram was also responsible for the abduction of some 276 school girls in April 2014, causing an international backlash and global condemnation for the attack, and in May, 118 people were killed by twin car blasts at a busy bus station in the city of Jos.

Mamman Nur and the Ansaru

Jacob Zenn, an analyst of African and Eurasian Affairs for the Jamestown Foundation and a consultant on countering violent extremism, distinguishes between the Boko Haram and the Ansaru, or Vanguard for the Protection of Muslims in Black Lands. Ansaru is an offshoot of Boko Haram and is based in northeast Nigeria. They kill few civilians and principally target foreign interests as well as foreigners, especially kidnapping them for ransom. The internationalist agenda is inspired by Mamman Nur, who was at one time a deputy of Yusuf. Nur hails from Cameroon so his interests may have led to his international perspective, but it was not accepted by the Boko Haram and he lost the bid for leadership after Yusuf's death. The fact that he was not Nigerian may have factored into that loss as well. So he moved on to Ansaru.

Like Yusuf, Nur blamed the economic situation of northern Nigeria on Muslim leadership who had rejected Usman dan Fodio's *jihad* but accepted a secular constitution. Dan Fodio, an urbanized ethnic Fulani (typically herdsmen), was a religious teacher who founded the Sokoto Caliphate, an Islamic spiritual community in northern Nigeria. When the British consolidated Nigeria and took over the area, the political authority of the caliphate was abolished, although the title of sultan remained and his leadership was restricted to spiritual leadership of Muslims.

Nur became known as an internationalist because of his connections to al-Shabaab, a jihadist group in East Africa, and to AQIM when he was out of Nigeria from 2009 through 2011. The AQIM and Nur coordinated attacks, among them being the bombing of the UN Headquarters in Abuja which killed twenty-two people in 2011. His international travel and his extensive theological training (more extensive than Shekau's) prepared him to lead those who rejected Shekau's methods and launched attacks on foreign targets within Nigeria.

Muslim Fulani Herdsmen
Another group that practices violence against Christians are the Fulani herdsmen, who have attacked Christian farmers in Plateau, Bauchi, Kaduna,

NIGERIA

Tarabab, and Adamawa States for a long time. According to Kaduna Governor Mukhtar Yero, Fulani have been "ungodly and barbaric" in the March 14–15, 2014, attacks on three villages killing more than one hundred Christians and destroying homes. There have also been numerous attacks on Christian farmers and village in recent months. Morning Star News reports that "in the past year analysts have begun to see some ties between the assailants and Islamic extremist groups keen to exploit longstanding ethnic, property and religious conflicts." Christian leaders believe that the attacks by Boko Haram and the Fulani are meant to demoralize and destroy Christians, and one leader believes that the pattern of the killings suggests a "systematic ethnic and religious cleansing." Some see it as an attempt to disrupt the country leading up to the February 2015 elections.

The national security forces cannot solve the problem of inter-religious and inter-ethnic violence on their own. God is aware of this circumstance and does not see it as defeat. He inspired Paul to write in Romans 8:35–37: "Who shall separate us from the love of Christ? Shall tribulation, or distress, or persecution, or famine, or nakedness, or peril, or sword? As it is written: 'For Your sake we are killed all day long; we are accounted as sheep for the slaughter. Yet in all these things we are more than conquerors through Him who loved us.'"

RESTRICTED NATIONS

TWO YOUNG GIRLS ESCAPE BOKO HARAM

Two sisters, nineteen-year-old Kamka and sixteen-year-old Naya, were sleeping when radical Muslims invaded their home. The armed terrorists entered their brother's room and shot him in the hand before demanding to know where the girls' father was. When they realized the two sisters were not married and their father was not home, they took the girls by force.

The Boko Haram terrorist group has declared war on Christians in Nigeria, frequently attacking Christian villages, burning Christians' houses, and murdering indiscriminately. They also kidnap teenage girls and force them to convert to Islam and marry Boko Haram members.

After forcing Kamka and Naya to walk through the woods at gunpoint, the terrorists immediately put them to work fetching water and cooking. A few days later, the girls were told that both of them were to be married. "We're too young," Naya protested. But the leader then showed them his daughter, a girl of seven or eight, who was already married.

"If we refused to cooperate, we would be killed," Naya told a VOM worker. "The man whom I was forced to marry took me. He picked up his gun and a knife and threatened to murder me if I continued to resist."

NIGERIA

The sisters cried and prayed together, unsure of what would become of them. But after two weeks, a Muslim woman took pity on them. While fetching water with the girls, she showed them an escape route and told them to run away.

The girls escaped under cover of darkness. They knocked on the door of the first house they came to, praying the owner would be friendly. Although he was Muslim, the man took pity on the girls. He allowed them to bathe and eat, and then had his sister take them to a nearby Christian village.

The girls were traumatized by their experience but are now doing reasonably well. Since it is unsafe for them to return to their home, they are being cared for in a protected Christian environment.

"I thank God that He has saved us from the hands of these bad people," Naya said. "Everything is now behind me and I'm not afraid anymore. I only want to look forward now."

And Kamka is also thankful for God's protection. "I am very grateful that many Christians pray for me," she said. "Despite what I've been through, I still have faith in God."

HATED BY ALL BUT CALLED BY GOD

Suleiman Abdulai is a Nigerian Christian who accepts the persecution promised by Christ. In his early twenties he became a Christian but not without opposition from his Muslim family, which urged him to deny Jesus' name and even tried to kill him, before finally disowning him. But, as Jesus promised in Matthew 10:19,20, the Holy Spirit gave him the words to speak before his accusers. And when he was being sought by killers, the Lord protected him. Although faith in Christ cost Suleiman his family, worldly possessions, and reputation, he gained everything by taking up Christ's cross.

Suleiman was born into a comfortably wealthy, northern Nigerian Muslim family. A smart young man with handsome features, he used his sharp tongue and fierce intellect to publicly debate Christians, trying to humiliate them. He thought frustrating the lives of Christians would help him earn enough favor to reach heaven.

His confidence in Islam began to weaken, however, after he agreed to attend a Christian church service with a coworker named Elizabeth. That first church service caused Suleiman to question his Muslim faith. It seemed that the pastor was speaking directly to him that Sunday morning, describing things he'd done. Suleiman was shaken. He angrily accused Elizabeth of tip-

NIGERIA

ping off the pastor. When she adamantly denied it, he decided he'd test the pastor. He snuck into the church the next week and sat in the back. Again, he felt that the pastor was speaking directly to him. "He said things that I never told anyone before," Suleiman said.

After attending only two Christian church services, he was persuaded that he had found the truth. He gave his life to Christ and began studying the Bible, telling anyone who would listen to him about his new Christian faith. When Suleiman's family heard that he had turned away from Islam, they confronted him. "Have you given your life to Christ?" they asked. Suleiman willingly admitted that he had, describing what he had experienced in church.

In anger and disbelief, his family asked him how much money the church had given him to convert. "There's no money," Suleiman told them. "I received the light." His family gave him a few weeks to reconsider his decision and called every Muslim leader they knew to pray for their wayward son. When several weeks of prayer produced no apparent change, Suleiman's father finally demanded, "Deny this religion!" But Suleiman replied, "No, it is impossible, because I've discovered truth."

The family decided to send Suleiman to live with his sister in Jeddah, Saudi Arabia, in hope that he would "come back to his senses," Suleiman said. After receiving a hostile reception from his sister, Suleiman left her house and moved to Mecca to look for a job. Though only Muslims are allowed in Islam's holiest city, Suleiman was admitted freely because of his Muslim name.

Any lingering loyalty Suleiman may have felt for Islam was fully laid to rest after he visited Islam's holiest site, the Grand Mosque, where the Kaaba is housed. All Muslims around the world turn to face the Kaaba—a square, black granite building supposedly built by Abraham—during their five daily prayers. "I saw it as idol worship," Suleiman said. "I knew then that Islam is not of God."

While staying in a camp for foreign workers, Suleiman heard about a man who was sick. "In Islam, it's not common to pray for the sick," he explained. "But I went to pray for him. The man asked me how I would pray, and I told him I would pray in the name of Isa [Jesus]." The man was so desperate for help that he allowed Suleiman's prayer, and immediately afterward he was healed. "I revealed to him I was a Christian, and that man took me all over Saudi Arabia," Suleiman said. "We went preaching together." They shared the gospel with anyone who would listen, climbing onto rooftops to pray in secret and meeting new believers in bathrooms where they could drown out the sound of their prayers by running the showers.

Suleiman soon decided to return to Nigeria and ask Elizabeth to marry him. After they were married, he took Elizabeth to meet his family, but they remained furious about his Christian con-

NIGERIA

version and his Christian wife. The entire family gathered around Suleiman as his father insisted, "Deny this Christ or be killed." Suleiman's aunts cried and pleaded with him, "Why can't you deny Him, or at least pretend to deny the faith?"

Elizabeth shook with fear as she listened in the next room. She was certain he would be killed right then. As the hours passed, Suleiman felt himself being worn down. "When the pressure was too much, I heard a voice," he said. "I looked around but didn't see a person. I heard a voice say, 'If you deny Me before man, I will deny you before My Father.' This is when I knew Jesus was there."

Confident that Christ was standing beside him, Suleiman told his family, "I'm not going to deny who I serve. I am ready to die, because I know He is here."

Sensing that the Holy Spirit was urging him to leave, he walked to the next room, took his wife by the hand and left his family's house. "As soon as we got outside," he said, "we started to run."

He and his wife escaped that potentially deadly confrontation, but his family soon came looking for him. Although he hadn't told them where he lived, they managed to find his apartment. One day while Suleiman was away visiting a friend, a mob armed with automatic weapons descended on the building where Suleiman rented a room. They searched each room in the building looking for him. Later, his neighbors told him that the men from his family said they would kill him when they found him. Suleiman said the realization that the Holy Spirit had led him away from his apartment that day gave him "the strength and confidence to serve Him with all of my heart."

After failing to find and kill him, Suleiman's parents disowned him and cut off all support to him and his wife. Ten years later, his children have still never met their grandparents. "Leaving my parents... whom I much loved... disturbed me so much," he recalled. "I am disconnected from my siblings and my community. After I gave my life to Christ, I would lock myself in a room to cry. I was not sad because I was missing them, but I was sad because they are not going to heaven."

Suleiman is now an evangelist and public speaker who lectures on Islam and shares his testimony. When he is not busy with speaking engagements, he spends his time ministering to Christian converts from Islam or others interested in Christianity. He simply offers them a Bible so they can read it, and then they discuss it.

Suleiman said he feels a duty to warn others about the false religion of Islam and to urge Nigerian Christians to reach out to their Muslim countrymen with Christ's love. He tells believers, "If I can change, there is nobody in the world that cannot change." In fact, most Muslims he shares the gospel with give their lives to Christ, but they are afraid to reveal their faith publicly. Like Suleiman, they are rejected by their family, stigmatized by the community, and brutally attacked by extremists. However, Suleiman has not been consumed by fear, because he is convinced that Islam is false. "There is no peace in Islam," he said. "Islam brings division, and the only way we can overcome Islam is by love—not by fighting, not by rioting. It is by love. If we can take the love of God and begin to share it with people, Islam will fall." He knows the gospel is the answer, but he doesn't think Christians are doing enough to reach Muslims in Nigeria. "We are scared to tell someone that Jesus loves them," he said. "We should not be scared. We have the power of God in us to reach a dying world."

This year, Suleiman intends to focus on sharing the gospel with Muslim leaders. "Anyone who kills me as a converted Muslim, his reward is double," he said. "But we will not be afraid. We will still preach the gospel to them." He asked that we pray for his preservation, but said, "For me, to die is gain."

RESTRICTED NATIONS

HOPE IN THE MIDST OF HARDSHIP

In 2008, Awuna Sunday began working as a volunteer at a hospital in Jos, a city in the northern part of Nigeria. Awuna, a thirty-one-year-old student, lived in a nearby village and started volunteering at the hospital to gain experience for his future medical career. He had been working for only a few days when he heard the distinct sound of gunshots ricochet across the city outside.

In Jos, Christians are frequently targeted for attack because of their faith. Awuna knew this and decided to leave for his village of Naraguta. It was just a few miles from downtown Jos, and Awuna thought he would be safe there.

When he arrived in Naraguta, he found the village under attack. Unsure of what to do, a thought suddenly came to Awuna. It was Friday, and he knew that the children of his church would be practicing for their upcoming Sunday school program. Perhaps, thought Awuna, the children would not be targeted, so he went to the church hoping for protection. After all, who would attack a group of children?

When he got to the church, the children were crying for help and pointing at something. Awuna could see a wire dangling from the inside of a powdered-milk can. It was a bomb that someone had thrown into the church.

NIGERIA

"I went to remove it from the presence of the children," Awuna would later tell a VOM interviewer. "I thought something would happen to them if I didn't." He reached down and picked up the can, planning to throw it through the window before anyone could get hurt. Before he could throw the can, however, the bomb exploded in his hand. Awuna was knocked to the ground by the blast, but he did manage to keep all the children from getting hurt.

For the next six months, Awuna was hospitalized as doctors worked to save his hands, badly damaged in the explosion. The pain was extreme, and as Awuna's body struggled to heal, his faith was also put to the test. During that time, Awuna was focused on only one thing: he wanted vengeance against those who had committed the act. He was understandably angry that this had happened.

Slowly, though, Awuna's perspective changed. Fellow church members came to visit him, praying with him, and reading the Bible to him. As more and more Christians ministered to him, his desire for vengeance was replaced by a nearly insatiable hunger for God's truth. Awuna admits that before the attack, he was not a strong Christian. Seeing how God cared for him through his persecution and the witness of others who spent time with him strengthened Awuna's faith.

"God gave me a second chance to live in the world, and I want to live it for God's glory. I share my faith with others...with unbelievers and with

RESTRICTED NATIONS

other believers. I share my story with them to encourage them even more," Awuna said with a smile. He also says that he has forgiven the man who was responsible for the bomb. The bitterness and anger that had filled Awuna's heart have been replaced by Christ's love and forgiveness.

Awuna did not face the challenge of recovery alone because VOMedical provided care and medical support to him for two years. Awuna is back now in school, and hopes to one day be a lab technician at a hospital.

VOMedical is just one of the many ways that Voice of the Martyrs is working with the persecuted in Nigeria. VOM and our affiliates are often some of the first people to enter a city after rioting has taken place. VOM provided supplies to the Christians and others in the city who were affected by the violence. Food, water, clothes, and emergency medical care are all provided in situations where violent riots have taken place. VOM also works with Christians in Nigeria to rebuild churches that were damaged by Muslim attacks. One church has been rebuilt seven times through the help of VOM!

Nigeria, we have seen, has a unique set of very challenging problems, but it also shares difficulties faced by many other countries with large Muslim populations. The issues are complex and the potential for further violence and persecution is very high. Despite a history of successful missions to Nigeria and the existence of large, fast-growing

NIGERIA

mega churches in the south, many Nigerian Christians, especially in the north and the middle states, face persecution. They live in difficult situations filled with religious strife and tension, and there seem to be no easy answers, at least politically.

Nonetheless, courageous Christians abound, many of whom have suffered devastating injuries as a result of targeted persecution and random violence. But the international Christian community has stood alongside these believers in their time of need, strengthening them through prayers and practical assistance. This is an affirmation to Nigerian Christians that their brothers and sisters in Christ do indeed care about them and support their faithfulness under such difficult circumstances.

RESTRICTED NATIONS

WORDS OF FORGIVENESS FROM PERSECUTED CHRISTIANS

"[My] family members that died, it was their time to die, then. Because even though they are alive one day, they will all die. Even the Fulanis that are attacking and killing, they too will one day die. But the important thing is that before they all die, let it be that God helped them to see what they are doing is wrong and they should change. We pray also that God will forgive them because [I] have forgiven them."

—PASTOR JOHN ALI DORO

"I would tell [the man who persecuted me], 'I forgive you for what you've done.' We see that in the Lord's Prayer we have to forgive those who sin against us; otherwise, our sins would not be forgiven. I have to forgive him and share God's love with him."

—AWUNA SUNDAY

"When the Muslims killed my husband in [the] 2001 riot, I made sure that I forgave them so that I can take the burden off my mind."

—MRS. HANATU GYANG,
who was left to take care of her family of nine without her husband (VOM provided her with a grinding machine to support her family.)

FOR FURTHER READING

The following resources are a selection of those consulted in the writing of this book and are recommended for further reading and research.

Books

Benge, Janet and Geoff. 1999. *Mary Slessor: Forward into Calabar*. Seattle, Washington: YWAM Publishing.

Boer, Jan H. *Nigeria's Decades of Blood 1800–2002: Studies in Christian-Muslim Relations*. 2003. Belleville, Ontario, Canada: Essence Publishing.

Crowder, Michael. 1962. *A Short History of Nigeria*. New York: Frederick A. Praeger.

Crowder, Michael. 1977. *West Africa: An Introduction to Its History*. Essex, England: Longman Groups UK, Limited.

Falola, Toyin and Matthew M. Heaton. 2008. *A History of Nigeria*. New York: Cambridge University Press.

Harnischfeger, Johannes. 2008. *Democratization and Islamic Law: The Shariah Conflict in Nigeria*. Frankfurt/Main, Germany: Campus Verlag GmbH.

Marshall, Paul, Lela Gilbert, and Nina Shea. 2013. *Persecuted: The Global Assault on Christians*. Nashville, Tennessee: Thomas Nelson.

Smith, Edgar H. 1972. *Nigerian Harvest*. Grand Rapids, Michigan: Baker Book House.

Articles

Fick, Maggie. "Nigeria Election Riots: How Leaders Stoke Muslim-Christian Violence." *The Christian Science Monitor*. April 20, 2011.

Human Rights Watch. "Nigeria: Post-Election Violence Killed 800." May 17, 2011.

Joseph, Yakubu and Rainer Rothfuss. "Threats to religious freedom in Nigeria." *International Journal for Religious Freedom*. Vol. 5:1 2012, 73–85.

Nossiter, Adam. "Vigilantes Defeat Boko Haram in its Nigerian Base." *The New York Times*. October 20, 2013.

Rothfuss, Rainer and Yakubu Joseph. "The Spatial Dimension of Muslim-Christian Conflict in the Middle Belt of Nigeria." *International Journal for Religious Freedom*. Vol. 3:2 2010, 39–63.

Taylor, Magnus. "Expert interview: Jacob Zenn – On terrorism and insurgency in Northern Nigeria." October 24, 2013.

Zenn, Jacob. "Nigerian al-Qaedaism." *Current Trends in Islamist Ideology*. Vol. 16.

NIGERIA

RESOURCES

The Voice of the Martyrs has many books, videos, brochures, and other products to help you learn more about the persecuted church. In the U.S., to order materials or receive our free monthly newsletter, call (800) 747-0085 or write to:

> The Voice of the Martyrs
> P.O. Box 443
> Bartlesville, OK 74005-0443
> www.persecution.com
> thevoice@vom-usa.org

If you are in Australia, Canada, New Zealand, South Africa, or the United Kingdom, contact:

Australia:
> Voice of the Martyrs
> P.O. Box 250
> Lawson NSW 2783
> Australia
>
> Website: www.persecution.com.au
> Email: thevoice@persecution.com.au

Canada:
> Voice of the Martyrs, Inc.
> P.O. Box 608
> Streetsville, ON L5M 2C1
> Canada
>
> Website: www.vomcanada.org
> Email: thevoice@vomcanada.org

RESTRICTED NATIONS

New Zealand:
>   Voice of the Martyrs
>   P.O. Box 5482
>   Papanui, Christchurch 8542
>   New Zealand
>
>   Website: www.persecution.co.nz
>   Email: thevoice@persecution.co.nz

South Africa:
>   Christian Mission International
>   P.O. Box 7157
>   1417 Primrose Hill
>   South Africa
>
>   Email: cmi@icon.co.za

United Kingdom:
>   Release International
>   P.O. Box 54
>   Orpington BR5 9RT
>   United Kingdom
>
>   Website: www.releaseinternational.org
>   Email: info@releaseinternational.org